Players of Shakespeare 2

Players of Shakespeare 2

Further essays in Shakespearean performance
by players with the
Royal Shakespeare Company

Edited by
Russell Jackson and Robert Smallwood
Fellows of the Shakespeare Institute,
Stratford-upon-Avon

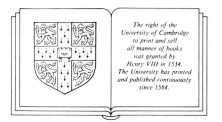

The right of the
University of Cambridge
to print and sell
all manner of books
was granted by
Henry VIII in 1534.
The University has printed
and published continuously
since 1584.

Cambridge University Press

Cambridge
New York   New Rochelle   Melbourne   Sydney

Published by the Press Syndicate of the University of Cambridge
The Pitt Building, Trumpington Street, Cambridge CB2 1RP
32 East 57th Street, New York, NY 10022, USA
10 Stamford Road, Oakleigh, Melbourne 3166, Australia

First published 1988

Printed in Great Britain at the University Press, Cambridge

British Library cataloguing in publication data

Players of Shakespeare 2: further essays
in Shakespearean performance by players
with the Royal Shakespeare Company.
1. Shakespeare, William – Dramatic
production
I. Jackson, Russell II. Smallwood, Robert
792.9′5   PR3091

Library of Congress cataloguing in publication data

Players of Shakespeare 2: further essays in Shakespearean performance
by players with the Royal Shakespeare Company: edited by Russell
Jackson and Robert Smallwood
Bibliography.
ISBN 0 521 33338 5
1. Shakespeare, William. 1564–1616 – Stage history – 1950–
2. Shakespeare, William, 1564–1616 – Characters. 3. Actors – England
4. Acting. 5. Theater – England – Stratford-upon-Avon (Warwickshire) –
History – 20th century. 6. Royal Shakespeare Company. I. Jackson,
Russell 1949–. II. Smallwood, Robert 1941– . III. Royal Shakespeare Company
PR3112.P554 1987
822.3′3–dc19   87-30909

ISBN 0 521 33338 5

WV

Contents

Illustrations

We are grateful to the following for permission to reproduce illustrations: Joe Cocks Studio for photographs, nos. 1–23, 31–3; Antony Sher for fig. nos. 24–8; the Royal Shakespeare Theatre Collection for no. 29; and Ben Kingsley for no. 30.

Foreword

The essays collected in this volume, like those in its predecessor, offer the actor's perspective on some recent Shakespeare productions by the Royal Shakespeare Company. In each case we invited actors to write about a role they had recently played and to describe something of the ways in which the work was approached. In one instance we invited two performers to discuss two closely related parts, those of Rosalind and Celia in *As You Like It*. The contributors had all talked about their performances in courses at the Shakespeare Institute. Some of the accounts were written during current experience of the production; some were retrospective. Our arrangement of the essays follows the order of plays in the First Folio. The writers differ in their approaches and emphases and in the degree of detailed analysis which they provide. Edward Petherbridge uses his performance of Armado as a starting point for wide-ranging reflections on the relations of actor, director, designer, and text which, in one form or another, lie behind all the essays in the volume. At the other end of the spectrum is the fullness of detail of David Suchet's moment-by-moment analysis of his encounter with Iago. In between these extremes other contributors respond variously and personally to our invitation to offer us the actor's story of the creation of a Shakespearean role.

In his Introduction to the first of these collections Philip Brockbank offered some general reflections on the actor's art and its relation to the plays of Shakespeare. Rather than attempting to cover similar ground here, our Introduction provides some description of the productions within which these performances existed and of their wider context in British Shakespearean theatre in the 1980s. At the beginning of each chapter we provide brief details of the theatrical (and in particular Shakespearean) careers of each of the contributors, and at the end of the volume we list credits for the productions they deal with. For the sake of consistency within this volume and with its predecessor, quotations and references have all been brought into conformity with the Riverside text edited by G.

ix

Blakemore Evans (Boston: Houghton Mifflin, 1974). Apart from that, however, we have tried to avoid editorial intrusions as much as possible, for this is a book in which actors speak about an actor's plays.

We are grateful to colleagues in the Shakespeare Institute, the Shakespeare Centre, and the Royal Shakespeare Theatre for their help in planning and preparing this book, and in particular to Sonja Dosanjh and Jill Jowett, respectively Company Manager and Design Assistant at the Royal Shakespeare Theatre.

R.J.   R.S.
The Shakespeare
Institute
Stratford-upon-Avon
April 1987

Introduction

RUSSELL JACKSON

T HE essays in this book offer the actor's point of view. They describe how roles were conceived and worked on by the performer, and the decisions he or she made about characterisation and situation. In this process it is not always possible to distinguish the relative responsibilities of the director and the actor, or the extent to which the final effect was shaped by the production's physical circumstances, particularly stage and costume design. This introduction aims to give an account of the overall design and effect of the productions, and to set them in the wider context of the RSC's work in the 1980s.

All except one of the productions represented in *Players of Shakespeare 2* were conceived for the RSC's proscenium stages at Stratford-upon-Avon and the Barbican: the exception is the 1984 *Romeo and Juliet*, which toured Britain (from October 1983) before a short run of performances in The Other Place. Of the eleven productions, four were directed by Adrian Noble and designed by Bob Crowley. Five directors and six designers were responsible for the other productions. (Detailed production credits will be found on pages 200–2, below.) Their work shows a variety of responses to the challenge of the main houses in both locations: in the Stratford theatre the actor on the stage is confronted by a broad sweep of stalls with dress-circle and balcony receding into the darkness beyond; at the Barbican the expanse of the seating seems even broader, but the balconies lean inwards towards the stage. In The Other Place in Stratford and The Pit in London the actor is never more than a few yards from the audience (no more than 170 in number). The new Swan Theatre – used for Shakespeare for the first time with *Titus Andronicus* in 1987 – has yet another configuration, in which the audience (about 450) is visible to the actor and itself on three sides and on three levels. Each space presents its own challenges in performance technique and design, although the large stages and the two studios obviously have much in common. Generally speaking, designs for the proscenium stages give audiences a greater degree of spectacle than is

I

called for in the smaller spaces: the configuration of the houses, with audiences for the most part facing a large picture-stage, is felt to require visual effects that are grander and more varied than some critics and actors would welcome. At the same time the actors are obliged to adopt appropriate vocal and physical projection to cope with the proscenium houses.

The Stratford main stage is equipped with sophisticated lifting and flying equipment, and can accommodate productions with multiple scene-changes, but these facilities are not often used. Partly for economy's sake, partly because of the pressure of production schedules, there is rarely more than one setting in each production. Sometimes the designer's scope has been limited by the lack of space to store and manoeuvre settings: this is especially likely to happen at the end of the season, so that the designer of the 'last show in' can find that storage space and flying lines and lighting positions are in short supply. The 1984 *Love's Labour's Lost* offers an example.

This design, by Bob Crowley, consisted of a 'box' formed by cloths, on

1   *Love's Labour's Lost*, 1984, designed by Bob Crowley (Act 5, Scene 2)

which blown-up images of parkland trees had been printed by a photo-graphic process. The stage floor was strewn with leaves and a number of acetate panels suggested puddles. Two translucent statues ranged up one side of the stage and a clump of umbrella-like 'trees' stood behind a park bench on the audience's right (Fig. 1). These could be manipulated from below the stage so as to open or shut – in the last dying fall of the play they slowly closed as the characters left the stage. This set was 'soft' in that the walls could be stored in no more space than a normal backcloth. At the other extreme in terms of construction technique was Ralph Koltai's *Othello* set (1985), which appeared to the audience as a black box inlaid with areas of light and which could be divided halfway upstage by sliding panels whose edges seemed to be neon strips. The technique for achieving these effects was ingenious and delicate – plastic sheeting held in tension on frames, with an equivalent of a large fibre optic for the edging – and the flooring and side panels took up so much storage space that a trailer had to be parked outside the stage door to take the overflow of scenery from Stratford's barely adequate scene docks.

The construction of these two settings is described here to suggest the parameters within which the Stratford designers work. The nature of the designs can be affected by considerations of budgeting or simple organisa-tion that have nothing to do with aesthetic, interpretative decisions. *Love's Labour's Lost* was 'soft' because there was no room for a more elaborate set made from wood and other materials. *Othello* was an ambitious box of light that needed the fullest possible resources. As with most Stratford main stage settings, the stage floor – which is looked down on from the dress-circle and balcony seats – was especially important. Almost invariably the actor is projected towards the audience on a tilted ('raked') platform and surrounded by scenery that competes with his costume for visibility. In some cases – of which David Ultz's 1984 *Merchant of Venice* designs were an example – the playing-off of actor against setting misfires. Ultz made the fabric walls of his single, permanent set so vivid that even the richly decorated toreador-like suits of his Venetians seemed lost against them. Mechanical elements such as the sliding lateral staircases and opening floor of the 1984 *Hamlet* can be impressive in effect but make the actors feel both insecure (they are afraid of falling off or being crushed) and overshadowed. It has to be said in defence of designers that actors are hard to satisfy in this respect: the parachute silk used in Bob Crowley's 1985 *As You Like It* was supposed to offer opportunities for a setting to emerge from the actors' work on the play, but the finished product, with its tall 'tree' of white silk centre-stage and a trough of water downstage, disturbed several perform-ers by occupying what they felt to be the best positions on stage. After the transfer of the production to the Barbican, this setting was revised, omitting the water and modifying the use of the silk. At the same time changes were made in costuming that reflected the actors' and the direc-tor's changing perception of the play. In this case the director and designer were able to get round the problems caused by the need for advance planning of workshop time, which normally requires a set to be under construction before rehearsals have even begun: actors have often com-plained that few designs reflect the work they have done on the play.

Some of the RSC's recent proscenium stage settings have been criticised as excessively spectacular. It has even seemed from some elaborately built-up sets that a revival of Victorian stage spectacle has taken place. A case in point was Robin Don's set for John Caird's 1983 production of *Twelfth Night* which consisted of a hillside and a realistic tree that filled most of the stage behind the curtain line: with slight variation in the form of park gates and a wall that slid on from the side, this provided the permanent locale for the action. Some critics thought that the striking picture of the play's opening scene, reminiscent of Giorgione's *La Tempesta*, was not worth the inconvenience of staying outdoors and under the same tree for the whole play. Terry Hands's 1979 production of the same play, with designs by John Napier, had also used a single, outdoor setting – scattered with snow before the interval, and even more wintry in the second half of the play. The 'twelfth night' of the Christmas festivities was taken literally. But Hands's staging used an open platform that allowed the actors plenty of elbow-room and did not locate the events in such naturalistic surround-ings. The steep hillside and uneven downstage floor in Caird's *Twelfth Night* meant that no one could make a running entrance or exit. Was this a subtle, directorial decision about the pace of life in Illyria or an accident unforeseen by the designer? All behaviour on stage is inescapably endowed with meaning, which it is the performers' and director's task to control: if the spectacle in this setting was at fault, it was not so much because it distracted spectators with what Ben Jonson scorned as 'shows, mere shows', but on account of the limitations it imposed on the rhythm of the performance.

In Bob Crowley's settings for two of the productions represented in this volume, *King Lear* and *Henry V*, impressive visual effects were achieved by simple means. In the tragedy a massive masonry wall halfway upstage swung back and opened up the full depth of the stage for the heath scenes;

Edgar's first appearance as Poor Tom was made by bursting up through the boards of the stage, which became a loft by the addition of a bare lightbulb; a shallow trough of water at the front of the stage was uncovered during the interval and a lift was lowered in the centre of the stage for Edgar to lead his blind father across a plank on his way to the imaginary cliff. In *Henry V*, described by one critic as 'a triumph of minimalism', the forestage was widened to make a long narrow shelf across the whole width of the auditorium, with the proscenium arch stripped of its cladding to reveal the bare brick structure; a white traverse curtain, some ten feet high, stretched across the proscenium opening, was manipulated by the Chorus, who became the presenter of shows revealed in the 'magic box' of the deep stage behind. In one of the production's most moving moments, Bardolph, Nym, Pistol, and the Boy waved goodbye to the Hostess from a tall, narrow slit of doorway in the backscene, Quickly went down a ladder in the forestage trap, and an 'iron curtain' descended ominously: a brief blackout allowed the French court to appear in front of this barrier, which subsequently became the wall of Harfleur, complete with scaling ladders.

Such effects are 'minimalist' in the economy with which they are achieved, particularly in the small number of actors (compared with Victorian reserves of supernumeraries) and the use of space and lighting. They are, however, spectacular enough to worry some observers who feel that the audience's attention is thereby distracted from some necessary question of the play. Recent forays into the musical by RSC directors and designers (especially *Cats* and *Les Misérables*) have been thought to indicate an undesirable leaning towards showy effects at the expense of meaning. Perhaps with *Henry V*, where the theatre's resources are a topic of the choruses, the distraction is felt to be more allowable than in a problem play or a tragedy. In this play the very fact of putting history before an audience is itself heroic. The production also used its staging devices to write a series of question marks after grand and inspiring effects, particularly in the final moments when the battlefield, with candles glimmering beside corpses, was seen through a gauzy traverse curtain behind the tableau of Henry's triumphant diplomatic wedding. Other designers and directors had used the full depth of the Stratford stage in similar ways. A series of simple, striking objects set in a sharply receding plane can have a powerful effect: one recalls from earlier seasons the sight of Fortinbras's army dragging cannon across the back of the open space in Peter Hall's 1965 *Hamlet* or the retreating line of smoking torches as Richard was parted from his Queen in Terry Hands's 1980 *Richard II*.

It is also fair to add that generalisations about the impact of spectacle are less useful than discussion of the interpretative manipulation of what is seen by an audience. It has been suggested that in *King Lear* Adrian Noble and Bob Crowley contrived an essentially 'transcendental' vision of the mad king and his fool in their first appearance on the heath, when they were seen in mid-air and in swirling mist, transfixed by shafts of light from the corners of the stage as Lear declaimed 'Blow winds, and crack your cheeks . . .'. To some critics spectacle of this kind is too readily an instrument of mystification. Others find 'an excess of pictorial invention' in the work of Noble and Crowley, who work closely together, preparing a 'storyboard' of the play's images. A definite sense of a Noble/Crowley *oeuvre* is emerging: water on stage in *King Lear*, *As You Like It*, and *Henry V*; a splintered stage floor in *King Lear* and the 1986 *Macbeth*; mirrors as entrances and exits in *Measure for Measure* and *As You Like It*. In all these productions there has been a readiness to explore each play's environment as a country of the mind. In *Measure for Measure* Vienna was a city formed on a crossway of two carpets, an iron tower dominated the back of stage at the audience's right and blue skies were revealed in the final scene as the walls of a box which could be entered through a huge mirror – recalling the pier glass in front of which the Duke disrobed himself and Angelo assumed his gown in the opening scene of the play. The Duke's narcissism (perhaps) and the looking-glass world of the play were objectified. In *As You Like It* the usurper's court was first seen under dust sheets, as though Celia and Rosalind had escaped to an attic; in the forest the court's chairs and tables were covered with white parachute silk unfurled from a huge circular aperture (the moon) at the back. This billowing material made a snowy, hostile environment into which the exiles ventured at their peril. Adam was in danger of being engulfed by it when Orlando decided to carry him a little further in Act 2, Scene 6 ('Yet thou liest in the bleak air'). For the sunnier second half of the play (divided at the end of Act 2) the white cloth was drawn up into a single column in the centre of the stage, and the floor and furniture, including a grandfather clock and a mirror, were reincarnations in green of those we had seen in more sombre colours in Duke Frederick's court. Corin and Touchstone sat on green dining chairs by the 'stream' as they discussed the relative merits of court and country. In the final scene of the play – in its Stratford version – Jaques made his exit through the mirror frame. By this setting and by casting the two Dukes and their entourages with the same actors, Noble and Crowley indicated that the country and court had more in common than their inhabitants might like to admit.

6

Of the two productions of *Romeo and Juliet* – Michael Bogdanov's in 1986 and John Caird's studio production of 1983–4 – one offered an exception to the pictorial expressionism of the settings described above. Bogdanov's modern-dress Verona was dominated by a three-flight staircase on a revolve in the centre of the stage, behind which images of contemporary Italy were projected in black and white on a series of screens. There was plenty of open space for the actors to inhabit and the play's social milieu was conveyed mostly by props (including motorbikes, mopeds, bicycles, and a red Alfa Romeo) and costumes. The surprises of the interpretation were events, speeches, behaviour rather than pictures. At the Capulets' party Tybalt (Hugh Quarshie) obliged with a saxophone solo, Mercutio (Michael Kitchin) played showy riffs on an electric guitar, danced frenziedly with one of the girls, and then jumped into an ornamental pool. Before taking the potion Juliet calmed her nerves by playing the flute, creating a few moments of eloquent, private stillness. At the end of the play Bogdanov cut directly from the lovers' deaths to an ironic epilogue in which the Prince read the prologue from filing cards at a press

2 *Romeo and Juliet*, 1986, designed by Chris Dyer (Act 3, Scene 1): Tybalt's red Alfa Romeo is parked centre stage

conference convened in front of the golden statues erected by the feuding parents: *paparazzi* and television crews scrambled for pictures and flashlights popped. The dead white of the stage and the bronze handrails on the stairs and side balconies suggested the expensive anonymity of bank and airport architecture, but there was no sense in which this was a Verona of the mind. In a world governed by the needs of big business (indistinguishable here from organised crime) romance and mystery had no place.

The studio production, directed by John Caird, was designed by Crowley, who brought to it his characteristic image-making. In a small space, and greatly aided by Brian Harris's lighting, it presented a Verona in which the tombs of the ancestors were always present in the rows of death masks fixed to the metallic back wall of the set: the tomb was quite literally a few steps down from Juliet's balcony. In the first moments the audience was presented with a glimpse of the dead lovers to underline the prologue's warning that their 'misadventur'd piteous overthrows' were to be enacted. Ever since David Garrick's version the prospect of staging Juliet's funeral has tempted directors: this production began with the solemn interment of both lovers. To one side of the upper level that served as Juliet's balcony hung a transparent cloth with an image of Christ; a cabinet let into the wall held both the friar's and the apothecary's drugs. The glistening leather of the young men's clothing, the glimmer of lamps and lanterns in semi-darkness and the subtle reflecting quality of the set's back wall created a sombre milieu in the night scenes. In Bogdanov's Verona Mercutio (Michael Kitchin) was a jaded, indignant realist, heavily dependent on the bottle and chronically hungover the morning after the party. His poetic world, corresponding to the society of the production, was witty, scathing but never sombre, except in the lines when Mercutio starts to talk about Mab making girls into women of 'good carriage'. In the studio production Mercutio's 'Queen Mab' speech, on which Roger Allam writes below, became a bitter, taunting assertion of the claims of one kind of poetic vision over other, more trivial perceptions: a fleering, dangerous night-piece.

Further, similar, comparisons between these two versions of the play might be made. The important point here is that the actors' performances were responsive to the environment provided by designer and director, who in setting up these conditions had suggested the direction to be taken by the actors' work. It is not always easy to distinguish between design that impedes the actors' exploration of the play, and that which excites them by opening up new approaches. The same discussion might be extended to costume, make-up and properties, which are to some extent more likely to be controlled by the actors' own ideas. It is now comparatively rare to encounter a Shakespeare production that uses Elizabethan dress: of the productions represented in this book, *King Lear*, the 1983–4 *Romeo and Juliet*, *Twelfth Night*, *Hamlet*, *Othello*, and *Henry V* used some approximation to the dress of Shakespeare's day. Designers seem anxious to avoid suggestions of 'fancy dress' or classical ballet: in male costumes breeches and jerkins (or doublets) are favoured. *Love's Labour's Lost* was set in the France of the impressionist painters; *Measure for Measure* seemed to be in the Vienna of *Amadeus*; *As You Like It* drew on current fashion; and *The Merchant of Venice* seemed to be in a world of Ultz's own making – half-accurate (Shylock's yellow cap) and half-invented (the 'suits of lights' worn by the young Venetians). Michael Bogdanov's predilection for modern-dress Shakespeare was evident in his *Romeo and Juliet*, which was set in modern Italy, with proper care for the observation of fashion – which may not be untrue to the Elizabethan view of Italy ('Report of fashion from proud Italy . . .' absorbs Richard II's attention). Sometimes anachronism is used to startling effect. In Noble's *King Lear* costume shifted to utilitarian, vaguely modern breeches, boots, and jackets as Lear's kingdom crumbled into civil war, but Kent's reappearance as himself in the final scene brought on a solitary figure in a stylish brocaded long-skirted coat of the kind worn in the play's opening movement. The *ancien régime* was suddenly recalled.

In some productions the use of music has been quasi-cinematic, underlining and commenting on the action and linking scenes more than has always seemed wise. Two examples: in Bogdanov's *Romeo and Juliet* the musical links suggested the episodic structure of soap opera; Ron Daniels's *Hamlet* had a more conventional score dominated in scenes of public power by clanging bells and in private scenes by a haunting reiteration of the traditional tune for 'How should I your true love know . . .'. In the comedies there has been a tendency to go for the grand musical finale, which sometimes suggests an over-anxious desire to make sure the audience leave the theatre feeling that they have had a good time.

So far this introduction has described something of the physical context of the productions on which the actors have written. Some of the most strenuous debate in contemporary British theatre is about the balance of power between director, designer, and performer. But a wider issue is that of the relationship between the actors' methods and those of the production. British actors are for the most part pragmatic rather than theoretical in their approach, and the dominant technique is psychological naturalism

9

tempered (more or less) by a sense of style. The recurring effect in most of the productions discussed above is a clash between stylised, expressionist staging and realism in acting. At its best the result is not so much a clash as a counterpointing of stylised and 'real', but it is fair to say that British actors are rarely expressionistic or stylised in their own movement and speech. When the productions are viewed from abroad – from the vantage point of, say, Ariane Mnouchkine's work at the Théâtre du Soleil – they may seem too verbal, with a lot of lucidly loquacious characters managing to lead a busy life in spite of whatever visual effects may have been contrived. Psychological verisimilitude and wit have been achieved at the expense of a sense of danger or magic. The visual and aural magic of the productions can seem hollow. To some observers, the RSC's work seems excessively reverent towards the text: others think that the productions pay it too little attention, and there have been suggestions that standards of verse speaking have not so much changed as fallen in recent years. Such critics usually hold up the performances of the company's first decade in the 1960s as examples of how Shakespeare should be spoken. It has often been pointed out that the RSC is a production organisation rather than a troupe in the strict sense: actors often return, but the number and diversity of the RSC's undertakings make it appear to be a not altogether coherent conglomeration of separate companies. The English Shakespeare Company, formed in 1986 by Michael Bogdanov and Michael Pennington, has been seen as a return to the company ethos of the early years of the RSC, and its productions of both parts of *Henry IV* and *Henry V* recall the ensemble work of the history-play cycles staged in the 1960s and 1970s. Again, in some minds large-scale Shakespeare has been discredited by the excitement generated by such small-scale productions as those the RSC has toured or shown at The Other Place, and by the work of companies like Cheek by Jowl and Shared Experience. Some performances (and productions) have been accused of offering studio-size work in a large space. The touring productions and the new dynamics of the Swan have made it reasonable to ask whether we should continue to call the larger auditoria at Stratford and the Barbican the 'main' stages. Are they still sources of energy and innovation, or anachronistic hangars that need noise and spectacle to satisfy their patrons? Preference for different kinds of engagement between actors and audience has fuelled this controversy, together with doubts concerning the social effectiveness and desirability of the expensive 'main-house' shows. But the power and subtlety of much of the work done in these larger spaces is suggested by the essays in this volume, and there is something to be said for the argument that Elizabethan public-theatre plays were conceived for production on a generous scale before large audiences.

There is a danger in this debate of seeming to reinforce the case of the governmental dismantlers of British publicly funded art and to discount the need for grand effect and gesture in the theatre's staging of old plays. There are signs that such criticisms as are briefly summarised above are being used constructively within the RSC. It should not be assumed that actors are indifferent to this or unconscious of the wider politics behind and beyond theatre politics. There is currently a heated debate on such issues as the composition and structure of the artistic directorate: it has been said that the power given to a small group of directors in the RSC distorts the processes by which artistic policy is formulated. It is also felt that women have too little influence on the company's artistic policy, and that there are simply too few women working as fully fledged directors in either of the English 'national' companies.

The performances described in this book have not been produced in isolation from the work of other actors, nor have they been evolved in spite of directors and designers or in seclusion from the theatre's controversies. Although they may not explicitly address these questions, they reflect the work of these actors, at this time and in these circumstances. This gives them their historical significance and explains (historically) some of their features. The essays also convey some of the excitement of the chase, the ways in which actors have been able to use the texts and open up new possibilities. As an institution, the theatre at its liveliest is always provisional, convincing for the present moment but admitting that in another time and in another place, things will be different. The essays offer a variety of approaches to the plays themselves, and give a vivid sense of the actor's job, with its varying proportions of toil, research, and intuition.

The Duke in
Measure for Measure
DANIEL MASSEY

D ANIEL MASSEY played the Duke in Adrian Noble's production of *Measure for Measure* at Stratford in 1983 and at the Barbican the following year. In the same season (his first with the RSC) he also played Sir Andrew Aguecheek in *Twelfth Night* and Joe in Saroyan's *The Time of Your Life* at The Other Place. He has appeared on both sides of the Atlantic in a wide variety of stage, film, and television work, including *Macbeth* for the National Theatre and *Othello* (in which he played the title role) for Nottingham Playhouse. Other roles for the National Theatre were in Pinter's *Betrayal*, Shaw's *The Philanderer* and *Man and Superman*, Calderón's *The Mayor of Zalamea*, and Molière's *Le Malade Imaginaire*. His many television and film appearances include *War and Peace*, *The Golden Bowl*, *Roads to Freedom*, *Moll Flanders*, and *Star*.

It was one of the most difficult parts I've ever played, but it proved to be one of the most exciting experiences I've ever had in the theatre and it has hooked me to Shakespeare for life. Almost everyone else pales by comparison.

In the first place, Shakespeare is the ultimate examination for an actor. He is imaginatively bolder, takes greater risks in terms of character and narrative, explores the emotional and psychological parameters of a situation more comprehensively than anyone else, and all this in a language of either poetry or prose as compressed, exciting, and complex in thought and feeling as anywhere else in the English language: 'high astounding terms', in Marlowe's lovely phrase. But the problems are further compounded, in this instance, by the profoundly enigmatic nature of both this play, *Measure for Measure*, and the part of the Duke.

It is curious. In many ways the tone of the piece is very 'modern' – ironic and ambivalent, characters and narrative rife with contradiction, the themes a complex mixture of political and moral ambiguity. And yet the function of the institutions at the heart of the play, like the church and the

13

state, have changed so ineradicably since Shakespeare's time that they can seem almost inaccessible to us now. God, in Shakespeare's time, was a living presence; you could be fined then for not going to church; suicide was the ultimate crime for the chilling reason that the culprit could no longer repent. In such an atmosphere a dilemma such as Isabella faces about whether to sleep with Angelo, condemn herself to eternal damnation but save her brother's life, is seething with painful irony and hair-raising moral danger. Today, some people find it in themselves to laugh at such goings on.

Again, in our democratic way of life, it must seem that the undreamed of autocratic power invested in the Duke is well nigh incomprehensible. He was King, judge, juror, and indeed the next best thing to God. And his power among his subjects would have seemed as natural and God-given as breath being drawn into a lung. So that the power of the play to speak to us

3   Daniel Massey as the disguised Duke with Isabella (Juliet Stevenson), 1983

now rested absolutely on our ability to recreate it as authentically as possible. It produced a tension on which the production thrived.

Without sound basic judgements, the instincts and intuitions in interpretation will be unfocussed and impaired, and I am sure that Adrian Noble's decision to transpose the setting of the play to eighteenth-century Vienna was crucially important to the success of the production. It had the indispensable virtue of retaining, still, an autocratic form of government. God was still an awesome presence. It imparted a sense of corruption and moral decay more lurid and venal even than that of the Elizabethans. There is much wit in the play, and the period is wonderfully suited to that, conveying as it does a sense of style and elegance, wit and ingenuity, intellectual curiosity: the period of Voltaire. Above all, from my personal point of view, it was a period to which my temperament and personality responded very warmly.

Power, in all its manifestations, fascinated Shakespeare all his working life. Indeed, it preoccupied him with a creative intensity unmatched by any of his contemporaries. Not just the symbol of power, but, much more importantly, the human face behind it. I believe that he applied the same rules to Duke Vincentio as he did, for instance, to Richard II. Both, in their very different ways, give public utterance to deep inner turmoil. Both are, palpably, human beings wrestling with the often intolerable burdens of kingship.

It is for this reason that I cross swords with commentators like Wilson Knight and Nevill Coghill who interpret the play as some kind of Christian allegory, and the Duke as some sort of Christ figure moving gently through the play dispensing pastoral wisdom. For one thing, allegories tend to create symbols of being, rather than human beings, in whom it is very difficult to inject flesh and blood, let alone contradiction or ambiguity. In any event, such an interpretation denies one, as I will hope to show, access to so much of the play's reality and unexpectedness. The play is, after all, in one sense, concerned with the process of healing, and, yes, there are analogies with the gospels, those great books of healing, which it would have been entirely natural for Shakespeare to draw upon, in the circumstances. But to make too close a comparison with the gospels robs the Duke, in particular, of a deep and existential humanity. I'll give one example of what I mean: in Act 3, Scene 2, just after the long prose passage with Isabella, the Duke is confronted with the sight of Pompey being dragged to prison by Elbow, the constable. There he is, face to face with a bawd, the potent symbol of so much that is wrong with his beleaguered city. Wilson Knight, pursuing his Christian analogy says: 'After rebuking Pompey, the bawd, very sternly, *but not unkindly* [my italics], he concludes (the Duke): "Go mend, go mend." His attitude is that of Jesus to the woman taken in adultery "Neither do I condemn thee. Go and sin no more"' ('*Measure for Measure* and the Gospels', in *The Wheel of Fire*, 4th edn (London, 1949), p. 82).

Now it seems to me that the Duke's emotions get very much the better of him here – conflicting and contradictory emotions too. Anger, that his city has come to this; remorse, too, that he is in part responsible for it. In any case, the anger is almost explosive. And I believe the text of the speech supports me here. The active, transitive verbs at the end of lines seem to propel him through the language with a kind of moral fury. By the end of the speech, incidentally, I used to seize hold of the chains wrapped around Pompey's body and shake him. I did it so violently one night that I caught the hairs on Tony O'Donnell's chest. And I have to confess that the sight of Pompey/O'Donnell's eyes crossing with the pain made a few repeat performances irresistible. I returned to my dressing room one night at the interval to find a Pompey bull nailed to the door on which was inscribed the message: 'O.K. Dukey! This is war!'

But I am, in any event, wary of the gentle Christ that seems to emerge in this kind of reading. There was a whole existential dimension to the man, born, as he was, to live a life on earth, with human appetites and human failings. I seem to remember that he overturned the tables of the money-changers in a state of abject fury. Whilst on the subject, I reject, too, the other side of the coin, that the Duke is an amoral manipulator of people's lives. I don't frankly think the text supports such a reading. There is a deal of plotting and scheming, it is true, but, behind the scheming, there is, always, the drive of high moral purpose. And to those who would argue that he is unnaturally obsessed with the necessity to make his scheme succeed, I would answer that he is playing for the highest stakes, playing indeed for his life and the moral regeneration of his city and his subjects. And in obsessions, ends justify means. He is, after all, dare I say it, merely human.

So, with decisions made about the basic political and social structure, the feel of how the play should be, what of the instincts and intuitions? I try to look for the reality and humanity. I suppose we all do. I found myself, in the previous paragraph, defending the Duke's obsession with the success of his scheme. Not as a justification, but because that was the way his nature responded to the situation. Who is to say, of course, that that is not the way *my* nature would have responded. Either way, I am encouraged by that impulse to defend what for some people would be a grave defect. Passing moral judgement, that is the curse, criticizing or manipulating from the outside, so to speak. For that could diminish, or even destroy, the contradictions of the character. I look for areas of the character that I can warm to, even love about him. In that way, you tend to avoid those out-of-date labels like good and bad. The person becomes more rounded as a result, more interesting and unpredictable. He will certainly be a person well equipped to capitalize on the ambiguous and enigmatic nature of the play.

Shakespeare, in some ways, is very straightforward. If there is something you need to know he will tell you. He is very honest, very 'up front' in that way. The trouble starts with what he *does not* tell you, with what he does not think you need to know. It is at those moments that the magical word 'ambiguity' emerges. And 'ambiguity' is a word with which anyone acting in the plays of Shakespeare must get on comfortable terms. It is, in my opinion, an essential constituent of any worthwhile piece of work. Shakespeare is a master of it.

In the very first scene of the play, for instance, we know *what* happens. Shakespeare makes it crystal clear. But *why* is quite a different matter. One of the dictionary definitions of the word 'ambiguity' is 'double meaning'. That is really quite inadequate. There could be a hundred meanings. A specific choice *has* to be made. You must use the evidence in the text, of course, to make that choice, but the imagination will play its part. I am convinced, moreover, that after discussions Adrian Noble and I had about the opening scene, I used my own personal psychological journey to heighten the dramatic tension of that opening sequence. I was able to identify very deeply with what we felt were the Duke's problems. It contributed to the sense of momentousness and urgency that the scene engendered. A gesture as immense as handing over the reins of power to a young and relatively inexperienced Angelo must go hand in hand, I felt, with some sort of psychological crisis. Perhaps it is an act of desperation. In any event, I divined, in that wonderful opening sequence, a passionate desire to put things right. Not only that, but also that he might have been planning this escape for some months or even years. A decision of that specific kind dictates a wholly different way of moving, acting, and thinking. And there was also, on Adrian's part, a desire to present the portrait of a man imprisoned in the pageantry of power, eager to burst his bonds, longing for the journey.

The Duke says to Escalus and Angelo at 1.1.67–8:

> I love the people,
> But do not like to stage me to their eyes,

and I tried, because of that, to present a shy and rather pedantic man. It would help to mark the contrast, as he develops a greater sense of self, of self-awareness, and confidence, during the course of the play. If, as I believe, his journey through the part is largely a journey of self-discovery, then anything that will mark that progress is an asset. And, of course, his assumption of the friar disguise is entirely consistent both with the character and the atmosphere we had been creating. It was a stunning visual metaphor. Dear Bob Crowley's designs were a huge asset here too. Indeed, as I stepped out of the formal black breeches, frock-coat, buckle shoes and powdered wig into the simple monk habit, I really did feel an instant sense of physical and emotional freedom. I say simple habit: simple but heavy and hot. I felt, at first, as if I'd slipped into an Allied carpet. I remonstrated with Bob, who turned those lustrous Irish eyes on me with the words: 'Have you seen it in the mirror? You look wonderful.' I stayed in the carpet.

It should be remembered here, I think, that the Duke is at all times impersonating a friar. He has spent perhaps an hour or so with Friar Peter learning the monkish ropes, but, in reality, he would not be above forgetting himself once he sees the disguise working. Indeed, early on in rehearsals, in the long Act 2, Scene 1, I found that I tended to get perhaps a little too close to Juliet Stevenson's Isabella, to be touching her even. I was actually unaware of it. But Juliet noticed it and remarked upon it: 'You're supposed to be a friar.' She was right, of course, but in a way it was a natural instinct. The other important thing to remember about the Duke/friar disguise is that because of the exigencies of the scheme he is hatching he becomes a very fastidious moralist. Where he is the friar, he abruptly ceases to have any knowledge of the Duke, and vice versa. He is wonderfully adept at shedding one or the other's skin, let alone his mind. It becomes the key, really, to the successful conclusion of his designs.

Once out into the streets, he is in fact responding to events, unpleasant though they may be, that, in one way or another, he would have been expecting. It would be true to say that here he is on a kind of pastoral mission, helping the walking wounded. It is not really until he overhears the news about Angelo's duplicity that the plot of the play begins to overtake him (3.1.96ff). At this point he becomes a reactor to Angelo's mounting treachery. The schemes, if we must call them that, are his unequivocal response to that treachery, a desire to save the victims from the results of that treachery. In any event, the mood and pace of the whole play is irrevocably changed from that moment. It is almost as if a bomb has exploded in the street. From now on the play itself is, so to speak, 'under the whip' and there is also a clock of suspense permanently ticking away on the wall.

But before we go any further we must examine the wonderfully ambiguous area of the relationship between the Duke and Isabella which is just about to hatch. It must be said that there is not one vestige of a syllable, line, or comma, even, until 5.1.491 to suggest that there is anything between them at all. Nonetheless, Shakespeare being Shakespeare, it is frankly in the air, in the journey of the play, too. And of course, at the end of the play there is this unequivocal proposal. It is easier, at the end, for the Duke, because of that, than it is for Isabella. After a lot of difficulty (we were uncertain right through the previews) Juliet carried off what became a little miracle of acceptance, quite superbly. Indeed, one of my treasured memories of the production was her performance. She brought to the part a wonderfully defiant and flexible intelligence as well as a painful emotional truth. I always think Shakespeare respected women. He was never afraid to let them think. He puts the majority of modern dramatists to shame. We found moments, of course, scattered through the play, where we could build a growing awareness of each other. Isabella becomes so excited about the scheme of the bed trick with Mariana in Act 3 that she plants an impulsive kiss on the Duke's cheek. There is more than a vestige of the adventure caper about the whole moated grange sequence which proved wonderfully useful, and at 4.3.142 where he must, in the short term, steel himself to put her through an awful emotional struggle, he plants a kiss upon her forehead. This is interrupted by the unexpected arrival of Lucio. They spring apart, and, in a long look across the stage at each other, during Lucio's bitter-sweet speech, much seemed to be accomplished. But the decision to bring them closer together was accounted for largely by the Duke's proposal at the end. If it isn't some prank, and in another kind of production I could certainly see grounds for that, then the moment, important as it is, coming as it does at the climax of the play, simply has to be filled. The Duke, as I say, has words with which to inform things. Isabella has nothing but her emotions. It is, in any event, an intriguing relationship, and Shakespeare, having greater theatrical wisdom than any other dramatist I've ever encountered, was probably right to leave the decision to us.

The mood and tone of the play changes at the news of Angelo's duplicity, in part because it takes on the aspect of an out-and-out suspense thriller. And the sharpness and ingenuity with which the Duke responds to those thriller aspects, saving the victims, bringing the culprit to justice, are the vital agents of his soft-discovery. The change of mood and pace is instantly registered at 3.1.151 in an abrupt change from the compressed rhythms of poetry into a hard-driven, free-ranging prose. 'Vouchsafe a word, young sister.' It is an astonishing sequence. He has to think fast and think hard. It is the improvisational quality of the scene that gives it its tension and drive. In the process he must gain the trust of this distracted girl, save her brother's life, while, at the same time, bringing Angelo to book, through the device, which he seems to pluck as if by magic from the air, of the bed-trick with Mariana. And all this, in two pages:

we shall advise this wrong'd maid to stead up your appointment [a pause for her to take it in], go in your place. If the encounter acknowledge itself hereafter, it may compel him to her recompense; *and here, by this is your brother sav'd, your honour untainted, the poor Mariana advantag'd, and the corrupt deputy scal'd.* (3.1.249–55)

At the end of this speech, if we had done our work properly, there was an audible whoop of satisfaction from the audience. The mounties were coming to the rescue! And all this in a man who, only hours before, was clamped inside his palace, imprisoned by his own power, seemingly incapable of embracing life or love, and powerless to help his subjects.

Fresh from this, we come now to the scene with Lucio. It is irresistible to a craftsman like Shakespeare. It accomplishes so much. Much needed comedy, for one thing. It advances the Duke's perceptions about himself, about his subjects and how they think of him, and for the fascinating Lucio it is the occasion for fizzling wit and fireworks. As to the vexed question of whether Lucio knows it is the Duke, I only know that if he plays the scene as if he does know, then the scene is as flat as a pancake. The scene, to my mind, is as perfect an example as you could find for demonstrating the magical properties of ambiguity. Does he or doesn't he know? Then the wit sparkles and the scene crackles with tension. If he does know, I am bound to ask what madness would then possess him, in the closing pages of the play, to tear the Duke's cowl from his head and unmask him? Lucio has many defects, but a passion for suicide is not one of them.

And then, as Lucio leaves, Escalus arrives upon the scene. Again, one marvels at the craftsmanship, at Shakespeare's ability to compress so much into the material by this subtle juxtaposition – the subject Lucio, revealing and infuriating by turns, and then his old friend, Escalus, a trusted adviser, the man whose gentleness and wisdom he had passed over, in favour of the flint-hard, cool-headed administrative genius. These are low moments, full of poignancy and even hopelessness. But contrast the following, with the thin and pedantic voice we heard at the beginning of the play; again, note the use of prose:

ESCALUS What news abroad i' th' world?
DUKE None, but that there is so great a fever on goodness, that the dissolution of it must cure it. Novelty is only in request, and it is as dangerous to be ag'd in any kind of course, as it is virtuous to be constant in any undertaking. There is scarce truth enough alive to make societies secure, but security enough to make fellowships accurs'd. Much upon this riddle runs the wisdom of the world.

(3.2.221–9)

As bleak and chilling a vision as you would dare to find, but within it, it seems to me, there is the thought, already, of resolution. A moment later, only, Escalus quizzes him about Claudio, whom Escalus would dearly love to see saved. The Duke silences him, the integrity of his secret moral purpose superbly intact. I find this to be one of the most impressive things about the Duke. The sense of moral justice that events seem to draw from him, and from which he will allow nothing to deflect him. It's as if he seems to be saying to Escalus: 'old man, you know me not'. The times are changing, and we move straight to the great statement of dark intent in the closing stanzas of Act 3. Comes the Interval.

I must go into the meeting at Mariana's moated grange in some detail. I think the playing of it gave me as much pleasure as anything else in the play. It affords a good demonstration of the benefits of turning the Duke into a flesh and blood human being rather than a symbol of Christian wisdom.

He arrives with some stealth to find himself in the middle of a scene of positively pre-Raphaelite romantic desolation. He is in a state of tension and excitement, for, at all costs, he must gain Mariana's consent to the bedtrick plan. The success of his whole scheme depends upon it. He listens briefly to Mariana's romantic musings, then, with evident relief, he greets the arrival of Isabella. He is, of course, somewhat embarrassed to find himself between these two women. However, in rather gauche fashion, he asks Mariana to withdraw, agog as he is to hear from Isabella whether the first part of the plan, the assignation with Angelo, has been accomplished. It has. Hooray. The suspense is immediately a notch tighter. He compliments her, of course: ''Tis well borne up'.

Then, in the next instant, comes the sudden realization of what he has yet to convey to Mariana. It fills him with a combination of panic and red-faced embarrassment, and if that can be etched into the reading of the line:

> I have not yet made known to Mariana
> A word of this

it can make for some wonderful comedy. So:

> What ho! within! come forth!
> *Enter* MARIANA
> DUKE   I pray you be acquainted with this maid,
> She comes to do you good.
> ISABELLA   I do desire the like.
> DUKE   Do you persuade yourself that I respect you?
> MARIANA   Good friar, I know you do, and have found it.
> DUKE   Take then this your companion by the hand,
> [turning to Isabella with a look of outrageous innocence on his face,
> as he puts her hand in Mariana's]
> Who *hath a story ready for your ear.*   (4.1.48–55)

At which point Isabella's mouth drops open in disbelief at having his dirty work dumped on her. It used to get a wonderful laugh, a wonderfully useful laugh because it brought us the audience's total involvement in the story.

While the two girls go upstage to talk, the Duke is left downstage, and it is here, in the text, that he is given a speech of some half-dozen lines (4.1.59ff) that seem to have no connection with what is going on in the scene at all. I am myself convinced that, at some point, and for some unfathomable reason, they were filched from the soliloquy of the Duke following the exit of Lucio at 3.2.184, where they make total sense, and it is to that moment in the play that we restored them. I knelt downstage, the while, in total silence and in the proverbial agony of suspense. It worked very well that way, and I cannot believe Shakespeare intended it any other way.

There is not much doubt in my mind that, if the Duke ever felt that he was involved in a play, he would be pretty sure that it was reaching its climax now. Mariana has acceded to the bed-trick and the rest is now, barring accidents, a formality. Indeed he arrives in the prison to greet the provost in outrageously good spirits, determined, once Isabella has arrived with the pardon, to bring Angelo to book in the strictest secrecy. From 4.2.79 he is maintaining the moral duality of the friar/Duke more fiercely than ever. But it is the further treachery of Angelo at 4.2.120 that raises the play onto an altogether different plane. It is this, I am convinced, that determines him to make it a public trial. Fuelled by a white-hot fury at Angelo's behaviour, together with the necessity, as he now sees it, to turn the issue into a moral crusade to save the city, it is this, hand in hand with the drums of the suspense thriller beating around him with ever greater insistence, that gives this section of the play its wonderful tension. The play is working now on so many levels.

And the Duke's first line at 4.2.129: 'What is that Barnardine who is to be executed in the afternoon?', which follows directly upon the provost's reading of Angelo's instructions, brings confirmation of the way Shakespeare means the play to go in this last phase. No puzzlement, no sense of pulling himself together, not even shock or outrage. The response is unequivocal and ruthlessly unemotional. He is out to get his man and nothing will deflect him. There are far wider implications now that simply have to be faced. For the Duke it is a stunning moment of self-discovery – 'What is that Barnardine?' – a growl of steely resolution in the mind.

Indeed he spends the rest of the scene steamrollering the provost. He simply will not be denied. There is no time to lose. There is some fun in it too. Here again, I must say that playing this scene with Oliver Ford-Davies's wonderfully impregnable provost was the purest pleasure, and, of course, by the next scene at 4.3.74, the provost, though he doesn't quite know why yet, is warming to the exigencies of the plot by coming up with the brilliant ploy of recommending the substitution of Ragozine for the recalcitrant Barnardine. The Duke's response of: 'O, 'tis an accident that heaven provides', to the provost's speech beginning 'Here in the prison, father', is one of overwhelming relief and gratitude, and it used to get a nice good laugh, but the groundwork for it was laid in Ollie's marvellous delivery of his lines.

Now, of course, the Duke has to move like lightning. There is the crystal clear objective at 4.3.93 and, a line or two later, the intimation of a much larger scheme altogether, when, at 4.3.104, he takes somebody else into his confidence, for the first time in the play. And then, in an instant, Isabella arrives upon the scene.

There is a story told by the French film director, Jean Renoir, in a touching memoir about his father, the great painter. Apparently, the young Jean would stand at the father's shoulder gazing with rapt concentration at what the old man was painting. He would stand there, hour after hour, amazed at the way the paint seemed to dispose itself upon the canvas without any apparent system or method, so that he was able only very gradually to discern the vision of the scene that his father had in his mind's eye. Then, suddenly, as if by some mysterious alchemy, there it was, laid out before him, symmetrical and perfect. It used to make him cry.

I've told that story, not because I would dream of comparing our stumblings with the great Renoir, but because the process of interpretation often seems to 'behave' in that way. A problem in one scene can often be eased by information gleaned from another.

It wasn't until I had worked in great detail on Act 5, for instance, that I was able to get on any sort of emotional terms with this Act 4 scene with Isabella. In early rehearsals I balked at it. Watching Juliet almost retching with shock and grief in response to news I had given her, that I knew to be a lie, was almost too much. But the Duke's intentions here are made, in the fifth act, very clear and very strong, the strength of moral purpose consistent and quite unflinching. But the germ for it, so to speak, begins here and it became crucial to understand why, for it lies at the very heart of what drives him through to the end of the play: the concept of mercy. Why does he not come crashing down on Angelo, and impose these harsh laws on the city himself. After all, he seems to be emerging now as a man more than capable of doing it. I think there are two important reasons. The first is that when Angelo falls from grace, it is a terrible blow to the Duke, not only on a personal level – the man is his protégé, promoted by himself – but also because Angelo, in a sense, compounds and intensifies his total disillusionment with the past. Not only is his city ablaze with decay and corruption, but the symbol of power at its head is the most corrupted and disgraced of all. If this is the moral centre at the heart of draconian rule, there must be a better way. Second, and more crucially, what the experience of the play uncovers for him is that he has, in him, a tremendous force for good and, even more importantly, the strength with which to implement it. In a sense, perhaps unconsciously, he sets the play in motion in order to discover this. The excitement for him lies in the fact that it was there all the time.

When mercy has such thoughts and feelings behind it, one begins to see lines like 'O, I will to him and pluck out his eyes' in a very different light. You cease, in a curious way, to be involved in the specific moment. You are looking to the future, towards resolution. I see in the margin of my script for this scene in Act 4 with Isabella, the words: 'He learns the efficacy of harshness. An indispensable quality for any ruler. Existential as well as Christian.'

Shakespearean fifth acts are notoriously difficult to stage. The various strands of the plot come together, each one thirsty for resolution, the stage is suddenly chock-a-block with people; where to put them, how best to focus them. In the case of *Measure for Measure*, of course, practically the entire city of Vienna is there. I thought Adrian Noble was triumphant here. He, together with Bob Crowley and Ilona Sekacz with her music, created a theatrical image that swept the play into its final pages with a combination of suspense, theatricality, and danger that served the play perfectly. I derived enormous pleasure from working with Adrian. His ideas are theatrically bold and brave, both intellectually and emotionally. He shares his experience of the play with you and invites you to share yours with him. It is this that gives the work its freedom, and breeds the confidence with which to project it. With Shakespeare confidence is everything. What I find difficult to accept in a director is arbitrary imposition. That is the handmaiden of fear, unreasoning fear, that most destructive of all human emotions. I certainly hope that the reader will accept that, for reasons of space, I have not always been able to celebrate the fact that almost everything discussed in this essay is the result of fruitful and fascinating debate between the two of us. I thank him gratefully.

But quite apart from the staging problems, the fifth act requires enormously concentrated playing, accounted for by the number of levels on which the play is operating. The stage is now peopled by accomplices to the Duke's scheme, some who know about the plot and some who don't. Preparations have been made before the Duke arrives, of which he is, of course, keenly aware. He is aware, too, as they are, that to succeed, the plan must work to the precision of a watch. And it is vital that all those who both *do not* know and *should not* know, MUST NOT KNOW what is going on. As if this were not enough to be going on with, it is clear that if the scheme goes according to plan, it will affect the psychological state of the main protagonists in ways that are subtle, grave, and complex.

For the Duke it proves to be something of a triumph, but it doesn't prove easy. Immediately he arrives you are aware of something new: the ringing tone of regal authority in the greeting of Escalus and Angelo, to the sharper ear, perhaps a little too fulsome. This is confirmed in the brilliance of his attitude to Angelo, fulsome there too, of course, concealing duplicity with superb confidence. With Isabella, too, the anger is almost too vehement, the moral outrage almost too strident. It is deliberate. Every effect here is calculated to rivet attention and allay suspicion. Notice the subtlety with which he eases Isabella into position:

> By mine honesty,
> If she be mad, as I believe no other,
> Her madness hath the oddest frame of sense,   (5.1.59–61)

and again, a few lines later:

> Many that are not mad
> Have, sure, more lack of reason. What would you say?   (lines 67–8)

There are problems. Moments later, his melodramatics force him to apprehend the fleeing Isabella, the stepping stone to the crucial introduction of Mariana, which, moments later still, is almost sundered again by the gratuitous interruptions of Lucio, leaving poor Friar Peter floundering. However, all is well, and in the wonderful scene with Mariana the tone is light and witty, mischievous even. Incredibly, he is enjoying himself. He is a master of light and shade, too, Shakespeare. Dressed as we were in frockcoats and breeches, bustles and lace, it felt, for a few minutes, as if we were involved in a witty and sardonic comedy of manners. But the Duke flatters to deceive. He is in deadly earnest. He has accomplished here exactly what he set out to do, the unveiling of Mariana, leaving him at line 239 ('Ay, with my heart, / And punish them to your height of pleasure') free to return to the tone of moral outrage. It is a wonderfully useful tool this, and he uses it with consummate skill:

> You, Lord Escalus,
> Sit with my cousin; lend him your kind pains
> To find out this abuse, whence 'tis deriv'd.
> *There is another friar that set them on,*
> *Let him be sent for.*   (lines 245–9)

So far, so good. A look to the provost at 253 ('Go do it instantly') and a look of gratitude to Friar Peter, moments earlier, following:

> Your Provost knows the place where he abides,
> And he may fetch him   (lines 252–3)

and the Duke hurries away to find himself or, more truthfully, to make the fastest quick change in theatrical history. But back he comes. One notices, instantly, that there is some similarity in tone to the Duke's. In any event he is as strident and outraged in the friar's behalf, as he was in the Duke's. Again, to the sharper ear, things are a shade over dramatized. He has, however, points to make, and more importantly, objectives to achieve. He

26

must unmask himself. He does achieve this at line 355, when, in the middle of a crowd of spectators, Lucio finally tears the cowl from his head.

At last. I remember I used to long for this moment in performance. The design so far has worked wonderfully well. But it is the integrity of this moment for which he has worked so hard. He is not to be disappointed. The tone changes here again, of course, reflected in the natural unforced tone of authority. No false histrionics. The rage and pain are specific though:

> Sir, by your leave.
> Hast thou or word, or wit, or impudence,
> That yet can do thee office? If thou hast,
> Rely upon it till my tale be heard,
> And hold no longer out. (lines 362–6)

The drive of the scheme continues unabated, however, always thinking ahead:

> DUKE   Come hither, Mariana.
> Say: Wast thou e'er contracted to this woman?

4   Isabella and the Duke (front right) in the final scene

27

ANGELO   I was, my lord.
DUKE   Go take her hence, and marry her instantly.
Do you the office, friar, which consummate,
Return him here again. Go with him, Provost.

Then:

ESCALUS   My Lord, I am more amaz'd at his dishonour
Than at the strangeness of it.

DUKE   Come hither, Isabel.   (lines 374–81)

It is a fascinating sequence. Short, sharp commands that leave no room for protest, Escalus's remark rudely thrust aside. There are important matters to hand.

Even with Isabella, there is a genuine and felt simplicity, marvel though one does at the superb control and nerve of the deception. There is always the importance of completing the task the speech sets out to perform:

DUKE   Make it your comfort,
So happy is your brother.   (lines 398–9)

In the great speech of denunciation, the sentencing of Angelo, at line 400, there is, as you would expect, the full 'celebration' of justice. He is speaking for his city, the anger, just and statesmanlike, the very scales of justice in perfect balance:

'An Angelo for Claudio, death for death!'
Haste still pays haste, and leisure answers leisure;
Like doth quit like, and *Measure* still *for Measure*.   (lines 409–11)

A presage of things to come? Because at this moment he doesn't mean a word of it. As always he is thinking ahead – to the mercy which is to come, to the irresistible properties of the mercy to come. To execute a man condemned in law by the edict of a ruler more corrupt by far than he was would be unthinkable. The tools are there. But he rejects them. Ironically, he seems for the first time to have found his true voice, and the fact that he seems omnipotent at this stage is, perhaps, because he is seen to be assuming the mantle of real power for the first time. Angelo falls under the spell at line 369, when he says 'When I perceive your Grace, like pow'r divine' but it is, frankly, an illusion. What is happening may have the aura of divine power, but what I think Angelo does perceive is a celebration, if you like, of the majesty of autocratic power, and that was the next best thing to God.

It is strange. I felt, in this whole sequence right up to the capitulation, if I may call it that, of Isabella at line 443, as if I possessed some of the proportions of Mozart's Sarastro. It felt as if I was subjecting them, Isabella, Angelo, and Mariana, to some kind of ordeal by fire. The sequence as a whole had the ritual of purification. It is constructed almost ritually. I felt, in any event, a thrust and certainty about what I was doing, a determination to achieve what I wanted, and the struggle to bring Isabella to her knees was quite literally exhausting. Juliet was wonderful here. In essence, of course, it was a battle of wills. Significantly, he is tougher and harsher with Isabella. Instinctively he knows that he must push her to the limit. He knows her well now, her passion, her stubbornness, above all her sense of justice. I remember that when she finally sank to her knees, I gave in to an almost trance-like state.

The rest of the play for the Duke is really, it seems to me, an exultation. This is specifically related, of course, to the unmasking of Claudio. Significantly, even as Isabella and Mariana are on their knees, pleading, his thoughts are rushing ahead:

> ISABELLA   Thoughts are no subjects,
>   Intents but merely thoughts.
> MARIANA   Merely, my lord.
> DUKE   Your suit's unprofitable; stand up, I say.
>   I have bethought me of another fault.
>   Provost, how came it Claudio was beheaded
>   At an unusual hour?   (lines 453–8)

He cannot wait now to spring the rabbit out of the hat. Having despatched the provost, he stands, eyes fixed unblinkingly on Angelo, waiting, the stage still holding the trance-like tension of Isabella's capitulation. Then into the focussed pool of light, the provost appears with these two muffled men.

> DUKE   Which is that Barnardine?
> PROVOST   This, my lord.

A pardon, for the first time. Is this an intimation of things to come? A stirring among the crowd, and then:

> DUKE   What muffled fellow's that?
> PROVOST   This is another prisoner that I sav'd,
>   Who should have died when Claudio lost his head,
>   As like almost to Claudio as himself.   (lines 486–9)

And with that, the provost slowly draws the sacking from his head, shaved now, of course, from the experience of prison, his eyes slowly blinking their unaccustomed way into light, the head beginning to turn, a look of puzzled disorientation on his face. Then, gradually, he and those around him begin to realize the miracle of what they are seeing in each other. For the Duke it is a secret he has held right through the play, a talisman, but much more importantly a potent symbol of the magical properties of mercy. Even here, though, he moves on:

> DUKE (*to* ISABELLA) If he be like your brother, for his sake
> Is he pardon'd, and for your lovely sake,
> Give me your hand, and say you will be mine.   (lines 490-2)

It is important to remember, I think, that the image of Claudio coming magically to life remains in the energy of the play as a very potent force, for the rest of its duration. I think it will exist in the life of the whole city for years to come, developing, perhaps, the properties of a mythological story. In any event, one's playing of the scene was hugely influenced by it, not to mention the audience's response.

My proposal there to Isabella often used to get a laugh. I never minded. There is more than a little chutzpah involved in the timing of it anyway. It is nothing more nor less than autocratic licence. One must surrender to that full-bloodedly.

Indeed, I think the coda of the play should be seen almost as if the Duke is settling his accounts with himself, his city, and his subjects. In a very real sense he is celebrating the re-establishment of an autocracy. There are instructions for all, including himself:

> Well, Angelo, your evil quits you well.
> Look that you love your wife; her worth worth yours.
> I find an apt remission in myself.

But, characteristically, the man is, after all, made of skin and bone:

> (*to* LUCIO) And yet here's one in place I cannot pardon.
> You, sirrah, that knew me for a fool, a coward,
> One all of luxury, an ass, a madman,
> Wherein have I so deserv'd of you,
> That you extol me thus?   (lines 496-503)

The Duke assumes the privilege of judge and jury:

> LUCIO Marrying a punk, my lord, is pressing to death, whipping, and hanging.
> DUKE   Slandering a prince deserves it.   (lines 524-6)

It cannot be shirked. It is the authentic sound of the arrogance of autocratic power, and it has returned once again to the city of Vienna. Whether it has returned to haunt it, or to make it proud once more is an open and fascinating question. Shakespeare doesn't say. He is too much of a pragmatist, too much of a realist. History has taught him to trust nobody and expect nothing. Predictably the Duke's last words are hugely enigmatic, and Shakespeare evidently feels no sense of obligation to him beyond the life of the play. But it is precisely these imponderables that give the play its extraordinary energy, that give it the power to make one want to return to it again and again and again. It is like a prism, from which you can extract a thousand meanings.

Armado in
Love's Labour's Lost

EDWARD PETHERBRIDGE

E DWARD PETHERBRIDGE played Armado in Barry Kyle's production of *Love's Labour's Lost* at Stratford in 1984. He first joined the RSC in 1976 and roles for the Company before Armado had included Orsino in *Twelfth Night*, Vershinin in *Three Sisters*, and Newman Noggs in *Nicholas Nickleby*. Among a wide range of parts for the National Theatre, and for the Actors' Company, which he formed in 1972 with Ian McKellen, have been Guildenstern in *Rosencrantz and Guildenstern are Dead*, Voltore in *Volpone*, Lodovico in *The White Devil*, and Soranzo in *'Tis Pity She's a Whore*. More recently he has been responsible, with Ian McKellen, for one of the companies at the National Theatre, and has added Lord Peter Wimsey to his many television performances.

'The words of Mercury are harsh after the songs of Apollo. You that way; we this way.'

As I write this it is about fifteen months since I spoke those words for the last time on the stage of the Royal Shakespeare Theatre in Stratford-upon-Avon. Outside there was a crisp January frost on the lawns by the river, though armfuls of daffodils were thrown onto the stage at the curtain call.

I begin writing these recollections on a hot sunny April day in a hotel room in Chicago. Far below, the loop train screeches and grinds along its elevated track, winding its way between the grimy warehouses that were here in the days of the gangster movies I grew up with. The carriages straighten into line as they run between the shops of Wabash Avenue, where yellow cabs glide beneath, in the slatted shadows cast by the railway sleepers. Out of the jumble of it all rise the immaculate dark grey lines of the tallest building in the world – but, let that pass, as Armado would say – 'A man of travel that hath seen the world.' Let it all pass; for after all, when the last gesture has been made and the last word spoken what remains to be said by the actor? The performance said it all, or as much as it was discovered possible to say.

5   Edward Petherbridge as Armado with Moth (Amanda Root), 1984

This morning, at breakfast in the coffee-shop, I was bemoaning the fact that my piece for this book was still only a series of rejected jottings, when a colleague at the next table looked across and said, 'I saw that; you were definitive.' (I should explain that I am here with the National Theatre's McKellen-Petherbridge group, though I do have a fantasy about being a writer in exile in my thirteenth-floor room.)

Odd; here was a fellow actor who had retained a strong, even favourable, impression of the performance I was struggling to write about. Perhaps I should set against it my memory of the dinner after the first night in Stratford, when my wife, Emily Richard, and I sat through the meal aware that our companions, all three connected with the theatre, were carefully avoiding the subject uppermost in our minds as we picked our way through a conversation with no mention of what seemed to be becoming our lost labours. It had been a first night in a classic mould. All the lightness and ease, the rapport with the audience we'd experienced during the previews, had evaporated. The sum of the production's parts had fragmented under the cool regard from the auditorium, as a green-room joke might at a vicar's tea party. The ground had to be regained. It was; remember the daffodils!

The audience is the additional character in all plays. First nights aside, it is a particularly curious character at Stratford, made up as it is of Japanese seeing Shakespeare for the first time and understanding not one word; middle-aged, middle-Americans catching the Bard as they might the crown jewels, or sampling the RSC as part of an intensive culture tour. There are professors fresh from seminars at the Shakespeare Institute; librarians from Salford and Saffron Walden; 'A' level students; German teenagers with haversacks, tired from the returns queue. What are all their expectations? What they get, usually, is a concept. Probably, that concept is over-ridingly a visual one. For example, one of the first things the *Love's Labour's Lost* company did together was to see a French film set in the late nineteenth century, because its photography had inspired the set design. We were transferring the play's action into 1895 and so, as well as coping with a text written exactly three hundred years earlier (full of contemporary word play and jokes, impossible to understand without looking up the notes), we were exercised in adapting our deportment and codes of behaviour to our modern ideas of 1895, in so far as that would, in turn, adapt to the imaginary court of Shakespeare's Navarre.

Now, the playhouse for the actor in Shakespeare's time was a place where the conventions of performance, both acting and stage presentation, were well-formed and understood. They were firmly supported within the actual architectural structure of the theatre which was not merely an extension of these conventions but an organic part of the very concept of putting on the plays. The great creative leaps which Shakespeare made are still there for us in his plays, in the working scripts his actors used. Oh to have been in that company! These scripts and Shakespeare's presence – his advice to the players – must have inspired his actors to develop a greater flexibility and refinement of style in order to attempt an embodiment of the delicacy, resonance and breadth of his work.

But, on the other hand, Shakespeare's influence made little, if any, difference to the way plays were physically mounted, and the acting conventions remained broadly the same. Everything Shakespeare achieved in the shaping and manipulation of dramatic action, in the handling of great themes, in the creation of character in relation to action, theme, and to society, 'real' or imagined – for all these dramatic achievements, the conventions of the playhouse remained perfectly sufficient. The opening speech of the Chorus in *Henry V* works on a magnificent paradox. It seems to deplore the inadequate means of the Elizabethan theatre whilst beginning the business of proving them magically equal to the task. The author indeed had a muse of fire. His plays demonstrated for his audience that there was nothing he could not cram within the wooden O.

Today at Stratford's main house, the season's work often begins with a new onslaught on the interior fabric. They alter the proscenium or perhaps move part of the audience onto the stage. At the same time, there is a constant exploration of acting style and a continually shifting attitude to scenic design. The directors are influenced by any number of traditions, fashions, and fads, from Brechtian alienation to commedia dell'arte, performance art, and the art of political protest. Social, even socialist, realism rubs shoulders with puppetry and video. The circus comes to town and the computerized mechanics are brought forth on the unworthy scaffold. We suit the action to the word, the word to the action in ways undreamt of in 1595. 'Think when we talk of horses that you see them', but soon 'real' rain drenches the actors at Agincourt. How superior we feel as we look back at the late Victorians, stage-managing the dawn in russet mantle clad with gas light and gauze, thereby rendering the line superfluous. They infested the wood near Athens, with real live rabbits – whilst a pit orchestra accompanied the action with the music of melodrama, despite Shakespeare's sparing and very particular musical instructions. However, since the effectiveness of Victorian incidental music was appropriately rediscovered in *Nicholas Nickleby*, the cello has sounded plangently between scenes at Elsinore and I hear that music underscores the love poetry at Verona this year.

At the beginning of this century William Poel began a movement towards 'purer' Shakespeare by attempting to go back to the structure and conventions of the Elizabethan stage, at a time when Sir Herbert Beerbohm Tree was arguing that, had Shakespeare's theatre possessed the potential to create the scenic splendours of Her Majesty's Theatre in the Haymarket, he would certainly have used them. Tree lovingly describes the interpretative possibilities. For instance, at the beginning of the graveyard scene in Tree's production of *Hamlet*, the scene painter showed it was the merry month of May. The birds were singing and the flowers blooming whilst the court mourned – an ironic juxtaposition – and at the end of the scene, as night descended and the organ played quietly in the nearby chapel, the cloaked figure of Hamlet returned alone gathering wild flowers which he strewed on the grave, collapsing in a paroxysm of grief as the curtain fell – thereby settling once and for all the vexed question of whether or not Hamlet loved Ophelia. I'm sure that the pit orchestra aided the reassuring sentiment of this moment. It is easy to recognize the absurdities and the liberties of earlier periods, but let us not forget Peter Brook's cut in his famous Scofield *Lear*. No flax and whites of eggs for Gloucester's poor eyes, an editorial snip which neatly edged Shakespeare into the pitiless world of Beckett.

Before coming in detail to that attention-focussing moment for any actor, the first rehearsal of a Shakespeare play with the Royal Shakespeare Company, I am tempted to go on looking back to the approaches made to the work by our predecessors. It seems that once Cromwell had closed the theatres we had lost forever what I think we all perhaps secretly acknowledge to be the essential Shakespeare in performance. This may, at first, seem unduly pessimistic, unless we admit that it is impossible to look back over the period between the reopening of the theatres in 1660 and, say, the Old Vic under Lillian Baylis without seeing it as inferior to our own in the interpretation of Shakespeare on the stage. (I have tried to suggest that the notion of our own superiority is mostly illusory, that is, if it were ever possible to conceive an objective standard by which to judge ourselves against earlier unseen productions.) We would like to have seen Kean I suppose on a night when he was sober. Although he learned his craft playing rubbish in fair-ground booths, the refined sensibility of his contemporary, Jane Austen, wrote of his Shylock as 'the most perfect acting'. Yes, to have seen Shakespeare in just one of those famed flashes of lightning (sitting next to Jane Austen if possible) – that would have been something. Oh, but what of the tawdry stock scenery and the mediocre supporting actors parading before us in clothes from their own wardrobes, doing the traditional business and making the traditional 'points'? It seems to us that from the reopening of the theatres the interpretation of Shakespeare was at the mercy of the actors, hamming away in traditional grooves with every now and then an especially talented performer emerging to crack the mould and set a new standard, a standard doomed to become a convention and then a tradition, honourably lived up to or slavishly and dully followed. But sometimes an actor would make innovations in what we now call 'production'. Kean's son Charles hit on the idea of darkening the auditorium during performances. Garrick introduced the splendid scene painter De Loutherberg to the London theatre. His designs were capable of forming the sole pretext for a dramatic entertainment and paved the way for the gondolas and canals in Irving's *Merchant of Venice* and ultimately, I suppose, even Tree's real rabbits in the Athenian Wood. It was Garrick who overthrew the sentimental taste of his time by ridding the stage of the happy ending to *King Lear*, and Macready who reinstated the character of the Fool. Perhaps the major influence in the nineteenth century was Charles Kean's, whose dissolute genius of a father tried to keep him from the stage, educating him at Eton. Maybe it was Eton which sowed the seeds in Charles for what was to become the basis of Shakespearean production on the stage right through to the first decade of our own century and even beyond; the placing of Shakespeare's plays in their 'correct' periods with, for the first time, carefully researched historical costume and settings. His influence spread indirectly as far as the Moscow Art Theatre, where Nemirovich Danchenko produced a *Julius Caesar* in 1907 which had the teeming period detail of a Cecil B. DeMille movie.

It was in 1908 that Ellen Terry's son Edward Gordon Craig arrived in Moscow to design and, with Stanislavsky, to direct *Hamlet*. Craig presented the play in simple plain screens, sometimes gilded, but most of the time almost colourless. Though this theoretically simple device presented technical difficulties to the Moscow Art Theatre stage staff, at last these screens, their double-hinged leaves closing and opening as the stage hands manipulated them to move on their casters through differing lighting states, created new moods, new spaces, and places for the action of the play, and for the audience's imagination to wander in. This near-abstraction arrived on the stage as probably the most sudden and radical change in the history of Shakespeare on the stage. In London, Beerbohm Tree was still reigning at His Majesty's Theatre. Craig characterized him in relation to the stage scene, as crying with Horatio in the first act of *Hamlet* 'stay illusion'. Now, in Moscow, the scenic artist's built and painted realistic detail had been stripped away. The resident stage designer had been sent away with his folder of carefully researched sketches of Elizabethan castle interiors. Clearly this was not the return to the Elizabethan theatre that Poel had attempted, nor was it pure abstraction, since the arrangements of lighting and screens were intended to evoke a sense of mood and place. Poel's solution had been the reconstruction of a theatre where the audience's imagination was prompted only by the words of Shakespeare and the skill of the actors. Craig replaced the immense usurping clutter of scenic illusion by a simple, suggestive kinetic setting, capable of making a strong interpretative contribution of a very new kind. *Hamlet* to Craig was 'a great dream' and even the new subtleties of atmosphere in production, and characterization in acting, with which the Art Theatre had triumphed in Chekhov, were useless for Craig's vision of Shakespeare. The production had its influence in Britain, where simple settings became popular. (Stanislavsky, as his notes for his later production of *Othello* show, went back to worrying about how the gondola should be sprung so as to bob authentically as Iago and Roderigo alighted, and, at the same time, implemented and developed his now famous System, carefully studying the emotional motives and the actions of the characters. Working on *Othello* on these two fronts, he attempted to produce a scenario which would present his actors with as few unturned stones as possible.)

In Britain, though Craig's influence can be traced right up to the Roman season at Stratford in 1972, with its moving square and rectangular masses, it was not long after *Hamlet* in Moscow that the first modern dress *Hamlet* arrived on the stage. It was as self-conscious a use of contemporary dress as the word 'modern' suggests. As long as the plays had continued to be performed in contemporary clothes, no problem had arisen through the audience's sense of historical perspective; but as Shakespeare the man receded into history, he was placed more and more firmly in historical context on the stage. As we know, the Victorians did this in a rather eccentric way by insisting that *Julius Caesar*, for example, should be placed even further back in time, beyond the Globe, in a reconstruction of ancient Rome. In the twentieth century our sense of historical perspective, as the world of Shakespeare continues to recede from us, has led us into a continual quest to make him 'relevant' to our own time, and the device of 'modern' dress is only one of a host of theatrical tricks we have used.

I come back to the word, concept. Directorial concepts help the audience to relate to the distant world of Shakespeare by shifting the action to more recent and familiar periods or by presenting the plays in styles which remind us of other playwrights or other theatres.

At last, to come back to the company assembling to rehearse Shakespeare at Stratford in such a year as the one I am writing about; when such a company assembles it may contain some actors who have worked for the RSC before, but it is often essentially a new, scratch company, which will possibly develop into an ensemble as it goes along. (There are many contributing factors to the relatively quick turnover of actors within the RSC but this is something I cannot deal with here.) One of the leading RSC directors said to me about three years ago: 'The RSC has never been an ensemble of actors. It is an ensemble of directors'! Rarely, however, is a season conceived these days in an overall directorial style. The 'ensemble' assembles to thrash out the play list; eventually, by give and take, it arrives at the list of actors and designers deemed capable of realizing the various concepts.

So, an actor might find himself starting rehearsals in the spring with a crash course on the trampoline. By autumn he or she could be perfecting a pavane. Regular voice and verse classes will have been on offer, interspersed perhaps with tap-dancing and tumbling. Some younger actors, perhaps playing important roles, may arrive unsure of exactly what an iambic pentameter is. To create anew the Royal Shakespeare Company year by year is a bit like giving a conductor three months to create the Chicago Symphony Orchestra. The extraordinary thing is that the directors and their actors not only often create startling original productions but a real sense of company, of (dreaded word) ensemble. Perhaps the late Roy Plomley might have offered his desert island castaways, in addition to the Bible and Shakespeare's complete works, the luxury item of a favourite concept.

Watching the Royal Shakespearean results, one has the impression of seeing two simultaneous shows: text by W.S., with accompanying pageant. Thrillingly, from time to time, the two shows synthesize, and occasionally this synthesis is sustained for such substantial passages that a revelatory effect is produced and we marvel how Shakespeare could have pre-empted *The Quintessence of Ibsenism*, or the dramatic poems of

40

Chekhov. We delight to discover the superb librettist of the modern English musical. Perhaps in some vague way we have a notion that somewhere there is another, purer way, without reverting to William Poel or making our contribution to the funds for Sam Wanamaker's reconstruction on Bankside. Of course, The Other Place began to explore it, though gradually the concepts crept in there, with designed environments for the plays.

With the advent of the Swan Theatre, the possibility is with us again of presenting the plays depending entirely on the rhythm of Shakespeare's language, uninterrupted by pauses during which the stage machinery alters the stage picture to the accompaniment of entr'acte music. Which is the more demanding discipline for the actor? Is it to stand on the bare platform so inspired of spirit, so well graced, so eloquent of voice and body as to be able to create the whole world of the play? Or is it to inhabit that world as it has been created through costume, set, lighting, music, and directorial conceptualization, whether imposed on, or 'discovered' with, the actors. We are fortunate, indeed, now at Stratford that the glorious possibility of both challenges presents itself.

As actors, we function at a time when we can look back over a huge spectrum of style and approach. There are some dear souls who regret the current lack of 'standards' or tradition. Theirs is a nostalgia for the days when the verse was spoken 'beautifully', in a perfect poetic blend of King's and actors' English and the stage was free of 'gimmicks'. There was no such time. The young Olivier was condemned for an inability to speak poetically, the young Gielgud was criticized for 'singing'. Before them, Poel was written off as a crank and Tree spurned as a vulgar popularist.

So, the cast arrived in 1984 clutching its plastic cups of coffee to approach *Love's Labour's Lost*, lacking for the most part a strong tradition and training in common; and, at the same time, sharing a lack of innocence from preconception – though of course the preconceptions were all different. Each had to commit to placing the first faltering foot on the floor of the rehearsal room, to hazarding the first sounds of his or her character's voice. At this moment the actor is at his most naked, his most vulnerable. In some ways he is mercifully so; still free from the trappings of the production which lurk in the corner of the rehearsal-room in model and drawing form. In an ideal theatre (there is rarely the time and money in the real theatre) there would still be time for *modification* of the ideas conceived in the director's study and on the designer's drawing board and during the dinners they had together, most likely before even the leading actor was engaged. Under ideal conditions an organic process could begin. There is no denying the astonishing successes, as well as the failures, of what I think of as the *un*ideal process; but it is a process often inexorably geared to a partial concept, which might embody, for example, a 'final image' to which any discoveries made in rehearsal must be sacrificed. And yet, and yet – theatre animals of all kinds are adaptive creatures and in the hurly-burly, even the chaos, of the gregarious collaborative process a kind of alchemy is achieved, even stumbled upon, despite the lack of a fully informed method or a surfeit of theory.

The problem for the actor is a simple one. I should repeat the word again with a capital S, a Simple and profound problem. It is the quest for truth, for belief. When Armado said 'Arts-man, preambulate, we will be singuled from the barbarous' or 'I have seen the day of wrong through the little hole of discretion, and I will right myself like a soldier', did the audience *believe*? In the end and at the beginning, the actor is simply concerned that his audience believe. He is concerned with understanding the truth on Shakespeare's page and embodying that truth in action and interaction on the stage – whether it be in rehearsal clothes without props and under the glare of fluorescent lights or in the most spectacular piece of director's theatre you can imagine. It is the actors who are the go-betweens for Shakespeare's characters and that other character, the audience. They are held responsible for nothing less than the words of Mercury and the songs of Apollo. This is the highest responsibility and the highest privilege in the theatre.

Chicago
April 1986

POSTSCRIPT   Of course, I simply cannot leave it at that. The equipment of the actor should go beyond 'the mind of a gypsy and the heart of a child'. Notwithstanding the contributions by actors to learned volumes (or perhaps because of them), there are many who still think of us as the precocious children of the stage, whose talent can be made to serve the theatre only with proper adult guidance. There is one British critic who actually traces the entry into the theatre not only of the intellectual, but of intelligence itself, to the late fifties and early sixties and the influx of university graduates most particularly from Cambridge. The theatre owes a great deal to some of those directors who emerged to influence it so profoundly, but there is a danger if this development is perceived simplistically.

University-trained directors brought more to the theatre than brains. The best of them brought more than an ability to read the texts in the glow of liberal enlightenment and show their urgent modern relevance; more than a rigorous attention to meaning and structure. The best of our actors, too, contribute more than charisma, more than flashes of lightning, more than thrilling cadence or unforgettably eloquent gesture. Actors and directors must learn from one another. To collaborate fully they should have a real understanding of each other's approach and skill. It is an understanding which is simple, and at the same time extremely delicate and sophisticated.

The alternative to this mutual understanding in the theatre is 'You that way, we this way.'

Shylock in
The Merchant of Venice

IAN McDIARMID

IAN McDIARMID played Shylock in John Caird's production of *The Merchant of Venice* at Stratford in 1984. In the same season he played the Chorus in *Henry V* and Tagg in *The Party*. Earlier Shakespearean work had included the title role in *Timon of Athens*. He appeared earlier for the RSC in 1976 when he played Don John in *Much Ado About Nothing* and the Porter in Trevor Nunn's *Macbeth*. He has also appeared in a wide range of modern roles for the Company. In 1986 he played the title role in Marlowe's *Edward II* at the Exchange Theatre, Manchester, where he is joint Artistic Director. Among his films are *Gorky Park*, *The Nation's Health*, and *The Return of the Jedi*.

> I digress
> Good
> Trust the digression not the argument
> I shall not pester you with argument
> Only digression
> You have had a bellyful of argument
> ('Don't Exaggerate' by Howard Barker)

Exulting in the fact that I had been asked to play Shylock in the RSC's 1984 production of *The Merchant of Venice*, I approached my first reading of the text with some misgivings, but not perhaps for what might be described as the usual reasons.

I was convinced the play was not anti-semitic and that Shylock was neither hero nor villain. I knew that Shakespeare was not in the habit of being explicit about his creations, preferring ambiguity to a hard line. This, surely, was why the play was produced and argued over in so many countries throughout the world, not least in Israel. The central problem, as I saw it, was not so much to divest myself of the paranoias, echoes, concepts, traditions of previous productions and performances, but rather how I might find a way to persuade an audience to do this. Regrettably few

6   Ian McDiarmid as Shylock, 1984

people coming to the play would be encountering it for the first time. The problem seemed less to do with my 'old luggage' than with theirs.

It was a relief to emerge from that crucial first reading, invigorated. I have always been attracted to the outsider. Here was his apotheosis; a proud, wronged creature embodying a passion so confused, so strange, outrageous, and so variable, that he seemed as triumphantly alive in this century as in any other. Shylock: the despoiler of conventional morality, on whose altar he refuses to be sacrificed.

I thought I understood now the 'terrible energy', which Edmund Kean was said to have brought to the part. Actor had matched character, volt for volt. Small wonder he left home for his first night, having kissed his wife and child saying 'I wish I were going to be shot.' It was clearly my task to find the raw passion of Shylock in myself. Only then could I engage with the audience and have some hope of displacing the weight of received opinions.

All passion is a risk. So many actors, by the time they are asked to play the great parts, are encased in such self-protecting armour that they are no longer equipped to play them. They lack the breath and the breadth. Instead of embracing the part, they find a way of keeping it at arm's length, of avoiding playing it. It is wrong for an actor to contain a part, he must open himself to all the facets the part contains. The central dynamic is to be found in the collision of the contradictions. I have long thought that the phrase 'creating a character' was an unhelpful one and not really what acting is about. My 'characters', it seems to me, have come about more by accidents of birth than by a process of conscious evolution. The building process – the ground plans, the foundations, the superstructure, the roof beyond which one may not aspire – owes much to an over-generalised understanding of Stanislavsky and is a by-product of the naturalistic theatre, where the psychology of the personality is the governing force.

Naturalistic techniques are not appropriate to Shakespeare. The plays aim for a distillation of life, not an imitation of it. Naturalism, or theatrical behaviourism, as it may more properly be labelled, is a formula, guaranteed to rob words of their value, to limit the actor's means of expression and deny those who people the plays their essential humanity and hence their universality. The act of acting is in itself the articulation of an intellectual and emotional response. Therein lies its vitality.

> I never heard a passion so confus'd,
> So strange, outrageous, and so variable
> As the dog Jew did utter in the streets.

'My daughter! O my ducats! O my daughter!
Fled with a Christian! O my Christian ducats!
Justice! the law! my ducats, and my daughter!
A sealed bag, two sealed bags of ducats,
Of double ducats, stol'n from me by my daughter!
And jewels, two stones, two rich and precious stones,
Stol'n by my daughter! Justice! find the girl,
She hath the stones upon her, and the ducats!'   (2.8.12–22)

It was in that extraordinary reported speech of Solanio – a speech alternately heart-rending and hilarious and sometimes both at the same time – that I found the roots of my performance as Shylock. I knew from my first reading of the passage that somewhere in there was buried the heart of the man. The speech in the weeks and months to come would provide the well-spring for the expression of Shylock's former, present, and future self and my identification with it. The first question, however, was how to effect the transplant. It was, as are all such operations, an intricate and complex one with the strong possibility of rejection at the end of it.

Before rehearsals began, I went to Venice, where I had a wonderful time and found one thing of use. In the Jewish Quarter, Ghetto Nuovo, I was fascinated to see that all the windows looked inward towards the square. None looked outward to the city and the sea beyond. So, I extrapolated, the Jew was not permitted to look outwards. He had no alternative but to look inwards. Light was shut out. He was left obsessively to contemplate the dark. Less metaphorically, inside were his possessions. His house was itself, and also the sole repository of his property: his wealth ('the means whereby I live') and his daughter Jessica ('the prop / That doth sustain my house'). Shylock's wealth and his daughter represented his internal life, 'ducats and my daughter!' and his 'precious, precious jewels!'. When they were stolen by the Christians, I conjectured, it was as if his identity and his heart had been removed at one stroke, his flesh torn away, his inside ripped out. At hand, to assuage the agony, was a sure provider of short-term relief – revenge.

I had arranged to spend Christmas in Israel – motivated again more by the desire to have a good holiday than by any need to research, but knowing that that part of my mind that was already focussed on the play would be alive to particular sensations, fragments, impressions to be stored, perhaps only to be discarded. In the city of Venice, the past seems so tangible that any intimation of the present seems anachronistic. American Express seems the ultimate absurdity. The opposite is true in the state of Israel, where the no doubt necessary (I saw the bomb craters) but still desperate, ugly modernism seems to relegate the great architecture of the past to a series of stage sets for classical revivals, some refurbished, some let go. To glance at Jerusalem's daily newspaper was to participate in the continuing saga of the Jewish people, battles and treaties, politics and passions.

Then I encountered Mea She'arim, an uncompromising pocket of individuality. Here, about one thousand ultra-Orthodox Jews live the life of the Polish 'shtetl'. Here too live the extremist sect called the Neturei Karta, who do not recognise the state of Israel, as its proclamation was not preceded by the coming of the Messiah. The men dress in long black frock coats, with tieless white shirts and let their hair grow long over their ears into carefully curled ringlets called 'peyot'. Their appearance is based on the fashion prevailing in Poland in the sixteenth century, when a king who wanted to attract Jewish commerce, allowed Jews to wear the black silk coats of the Gentile free-traders in the country. My thoughts turned to Shylock's 'Jewish gaberdine', the distinctive mantle the Jew was permitted to wear but usually disfigured in some way by the compulsory red or yellow badge, 'for suff'rance is the badge of all our tribe'. The coat would indicate the tribe – Tubal should have one too – and the badge would be glaring evidence of Christian oppression. Perhaps it should be a hat; not fur-lined or a homberg like the fiercely dignified inhabitants of Mea She'arim, but something shaming, more grotesque, like a dunce's cap. My visual imagination had been excited, over-excited perhaps. Were these neo-conservative Jews anything to do with Shylock? Certainly they hailed from sixteenth-century Middle Europe. Where was Shakespeare's Jew from? Was he necessarily an Italian Jew? To the Christians he was an 'alien', an immigrant in every sense. 'A diamond gone, cost me two thousand ducats in Frankfurt!' Did he hail from Germany, I speculated; funnelled, as so many had been, from free cities into imprisoning ghettos where they were to remain, fossilised, for years? The question of whether or not to use an accent had vexed me. It was clear that Shylock's language was unlike that of anyone else in the play. 'And *spet* upon my Jewish gaberdine.' Was this an indication of some accent or a felicitous misprint? If an accent were to be employed, German seemed quite appropriate, but a bastardised German. All around me there was the evocative sing-song sound of Yiddish, the language frowned on by some but spoken by many who regard Hebrew as a holy language to be used only in prayer. Yiddish: the language of the ghetto, but, no doubt because of its origin, a language of great energy. It has the potency and self-deprecating humour, born of years of oppression.

This, I was now convinced, should be the accent of Shakespeare's bastard Venetian.

I allowed the discovery to act on me as I made my way past the synagogues and Talmudic academies, through Zion Square, past the old Italian Hospital, and back to the Old City and my hotel. The Sabbath was approaching. Soon all work in Mea She'arim would stop and visitors would no longer be welcome. Here I was, an alien in a society whose religion, pleasures, aims, and attitudes were radically different from my own. This was Shylock's state in Christian Venice. But I was only passing through, a voyeur, a tourist day-tripping in other people's lives, an actor. The mind now clogged with impressions, it was time to return to the play.

I had made one stipulation when I accepted the part: the production should be set in Renaissance Venice rather than in a period and a location which might emphasise some of the play's themes at the expense of others. 'Period' or modern dress productions of Shakespeare, while often successful in creating a strong social framework for the plays, can often distort the text and diminish the possibilities of choice for the actor, being an impediment rather than a stimulant to the imagination. There was much to admire in Jonathan Miller's television version of his National Theatre production of the play. A café setting seemed quite appropriate for the opening scene but when I felt I recognised it as Florian's on St Mark's Square, it seemed as anachronistic as American Express and at odds with the world of the play. The setting also seemed to demand a naturalism which the verse could not sustain. An attempt to pin down an idea had resulted in a jarring oversimplification.

David Ultz, our designer, understood and was responsive to all this. He wanted to achieve Shakespeare's Venice filtered through his contemporary imagination. It is, alas, a long and bumpy journey from the inception to the execution, and while Ultz's design had very strong reverberations for himself and the director, it proved distracting and unwieldy for actors and audiences. The set was a large square room defined entirely by curtains and a carpet, with two 'practical' organs and two 'practising' organists at either side. The room was to serve as both Venice and Belmont. It succeeded in evoking neither. It failed ultimately because it tried to do the work of the text and the actors, rather than provide an architecture or a way of using the stage-space, in which the text and the actors could work. In mistakenly feeling he had to provide an interpretation, he had, unintentionally, created an imposition. The design, however, made some sense in Act 1, Scene 3. I could imagine that on the one day he has need of him, Antonio, the merchant, might invite Shylock, the usurer, to do business with him in an opulent salon; a monument to wealth and privilege, emphasising how money had become a form of social power in this mercantile economy. A dunce's cap peeped through the curtained walls. 'Three thousand ducats – well.' The Jew stands in traditional garb, black silk coat, red hair, ringlets, his beard shaped, as if to emphasise his vulpine features, blinking in amazement at this Aladdin's cave of capitalism. The exotic outsider is permitted a glimpse of 'civilised' Christian society. Allowed, for once, to remove his ugly yellow 'badge', he reveals his 'yarmulke' and gleefully sets about subverting the conventional morality, satirising the hypocrisy of 'Christian values' in terms of profit and loss.

SHYLOCK   Antonio is a good man.
BASSANIO   Have you heard any imputation to the contrary?
SHYLOCK   Ho no, no, no, no! My meaning in saying he is a good man is to have you
understand me that he is sufficient.   (1.3.12–17)

The 'good man' appears and Shylock breaks out of the scene (almost out of the play) to inform the audience of his true feelings. In one of the most arresting of soliloquies (lines 41ff), he unashamedly regales us with his loathing of Antonio and affirms his determination to pursue any avenue that may lead to his entrapment.

> I hate him for he is a Christian . . .
> If I can catch him once upon the hip,
> I will feed fat the ancient grudge I bear him . . .
> . . . Cursed be my tribe
> If I forgive him!

Having required Antonio to listen to the theory of usury expounded from the point of view of Judaism (the 'Laban' speech) liberally sprinkled with self-parody and sexual innuendo, and having been infuriated by Antonio's response, 'The devil can cite Scripture for his purpose' (line 98), Shylock in a moment of brilliant improvisation invents the 'merry bond'; a skilful parody of the Aristotelian argument that money is barren and cannot breed money. 'This is kind I offer' (line 142). Antonio recognises the game and responds accordingly,

> Content, in faith, I'll seal to such a bond,
> And say there is much kindness in the Jew.   (lines 152–3)

Shylock, heady with his first flirtation with power, leaves for home with the words, 'I'll be with you' (line 177), suggesting what would have previously been unthinkable, that he and Antonio are equals. But the merchant has the last word, 'Hie thee, gentle Jew' (line 178) – the last play on words in the scene, with their prophetic echo of what is to become the Jew's final humiliation, his enforced conversion to Christianity. In the court scene, the word-play is translated into cruel reality for the Jew and for the merchant.

In Act 2, Scene 5, we find Shylock on home ground. We set the scene inside rather than 'before' Shylock's house as some texts indicate; a confined space, confining the Jew, his daughter, and his servant. Launcelot is leaving his master for Bassanio. Soon after, Jessica will leave her father for Lorenzo. In our production, Shylock had clearly just come from prayer and meditation, displaying some of his accumulated wealth – his rings. His relationship with his daughter seemed to me a familiar one. He loved her deeply, was bewildered by her youth and was dependent on her as housekeeper, confidante, and friend. He behaved towards her as he had perhaps behaved towards her mother, the adored Leah, but having to remind himself, perhaps a little regretfully, that Jessica was his daughter, not his wife. Before leaving for his meal he folds his prayer shawl and gives Jessica his rings (at the time, Jews were not permitted to display any public signs of wealth), almost forgetting to remove his most prized possession – Leah's turquoise. With a surge of melancholy, he embraces his daughter, unwittingly for the last time. 'Fast bind, fast find' (line 54). Soon Jessica will no longer exist for him, except – like Leah – as a memory to burn his heart.

The conversation of Solanio and Salerio, including that great reported speech, prepares us for Shylock's transformation. He enters in the first scene of Act 3, dragging his gown, hair unkempt, half crazed with grief, fury, and exhaustion and encounters the two Christian sycophants. 'You *knew*' (line 24). Suddenly it all becomes clear. Something in Solanio's tone brings everything into focus. The Christian plot to steal his daughter was a premeditated act.

In early rehearsals I was puzzled as to why Shylock had wasted his breath on these two insufferable Venetians. Later I saw the connection with the first scene. Shylock once again employs 'Christian tactics'. As you treat me, so I will treat you. 'The villainy you teach me, I will execute' (line 71). The theft of his money and jewels, the 'murder' (for she was now dead to him) of his daughter would be matched with an act of equal barbarism. These are no more than disorganised thoughts in Shylock's head at the beginning of the scene. By its close and, after what really amounts to a nervous breakdown in front of Tubal, his friend and confessor, he reconstitutes himself and decides to use the Christian law to enshrine an act of murder. The irony and parody we saw in the first scene have now, like Shylock himself, reached grotesque proportions. The Jew's Satire has become the Jew's Drama of Revenge.

We next see him parodying the parody:

> Thou call'dst me dog before thou hadst a cause,
> But since I am a dog, beware my fangs. (3.3.6–7)

Shylock, treated, spurned, and kicked as a dog, to protect himself, becomes a dog, ending on all fours before the Duke. By the end of the court scene, the Jew's Drama of Revenge has become his Tragedy.

I have chosen not to write in detail about the two 'famous' scenes (Act 3, Scene 1, and Act 4, Scene 1). I think enough has been written about them. Suffice it to say that my approach to them was – like Shylock's – emotional rather than intellectual.

That the 1984 Stratford production of *The Merchant of Venice* was

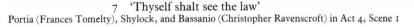

7 'Thyself shalt see the law'
Portia (Frances Tomelty), Shylock, and Bassanio (Christopher Ravenscroft) in Act 4, Scene 1

unsatisfactory is a fact with which few will quarrel. My performance was the subject of much controversy. Controversy will never be far away whenever this play is performed. Shylock remains, indisputably, a figure of great energy and passion and like all such figures arouses sharply conflicting emotions perhaps most of all in those who lack his dynamism. He may be a 'dog' but he's no domestic. He disrupts harmony and confuses morality. In that he is perhaps not unlike that other archetypal outsider, the actor. But, I digress.

Celia and Rosalind in
As You Like It

FIONA SHAW and JULIET STEVENSON

IONA SHAW and JULIET STEVENSON played Celia and Rosalind in Adrian Noble's production of *As You Like It* at Stratford in 1985 and at the Barbican the following year. As well as Celia, Fiona Shaw also played in that season Tatiana in Gorky's *The Philistines* and Mme de Volanges in *Les Liaisons Dangereuses*, adding Erika Bruckner in *Mephisto* at the Barbican the following year. This was her first season with the RSC. Earlier work had included Rosaline in *Love's Labour's Lost* and, at the National Theatre, Julia in *The Rivals*. In 1986–7 she played Portia in *The Merchant of Venice* and Beatrice in *Much Ado About Nothing* on the RSC's regional tour, returning to Stratford for the 1987 season to play Katherina in *The Taming of the Shrew*, Mistress Carol in Shirley's *Hyde Park*, and Lady Frample in Jonson's *The New Inn*. Her television performances have been in *Fireworks for Elspeth*, *Sacred Hearts*, and *Love Story*. As well as Rosalind, Juliet Stevenson's roles at Stratford in 1985 were Cressida and the Présidente de Tourvel in *Les Liaisons Dangereuses*. Her first year with the RSC was 1978 when a variety of roles included that of Octavia in Peter Brook's production of *Antony and Cleopatra*. In 1980 she played Lady Percy in the RSC's regional tour of *1 and 2 Henry IV* and the following year she returned to Stratford to play Hippolyta and Titania, Susan in *The Witch of Edmonton*, and Clara Douglas in *Money*. In 1983 she played Isabella in *Measure for Measure* (opposite Daniel Massey's Duke of Vienna). Other recent stage performances include the title role in Lorca's *Yerma* at the National Theatre. On television she has played in *Time out of Mind*, *Maybury*, *Freud*, and the title role in *Antigone*.

Any actress embarking on a production of *As You Like It* is embarking on a voyage of discovery. This is, of course, true of all plays and productions, but it is our experience that this particular voyage led us into a terrain more demanding, exhilarating, and enriching than either of us had previously known. Like Rosalind and Celia encountering the Forest of Arden for the first time, we found the play to be, for us, an uncharted territory – one that afforded boundless areas for exploration, but whose horizon was continually out of reach. To write about the play in full, or about Rosalind alone, would require more space than this chapter allows, so it is upon our *combined* journey through rehearsal and performance that we have decided to focus, concentrating primarily on the friendship between the two women and its resonance in the play as a whole.

It was clear from the first day of rehearsal that what is written is a remarkable and unusual relationship, for which there are few parallels in Shakespeare, with the possible exception of Helena and Hermia in *A Midsummer Night's Dream*. He writes of female friendship, but rarely between women of the same age and status, and the women are never so centrally placed in the play. We soon discovered a mutual interest in redefining that friendship, sharing as we did a frustration about the portrayal of female friendships on stage. It often seems that the audience's

8   Fiona Shaw as Celia and Juliet Stevenson as Rosalind, 1985

relish of that friendship is based on the actresses' working in *spite* of each other – the kind of traditional 'feminine behaviour' which is based on divisiveness rather than bonding. Armed with this resolve to jettison stereotype, we began work – a resolve already aided, incidentally, by Adrian Noble having cast a Celia two inches *taller* than her Rosalind, thereby forcing the audience to abandon any preconceptions about 'the tall skinny one and the little dumpy one'. Another decision he had already made was to set the production in modern dress, which we both also welcomed, for although such a decision can bring with it certain attendant pitfalls, it nevertheless obliges both audience and actors to recognise the play in the light of contemporary thinking and experience. To liberate Shakespeare's women from the confines of literary and theatrical tradition requires an analysis of the nature and effects of those social structures which define and contain them – the opening of this play sees Rosalind and Celia already contained within a structure that is oppressive and patriarchal, namely the court of Duke Frederick, Celia's father. The modern dress decision served to remind us that such structures are by no means 'ancient history', and that the freedom and self-definition that the two girls are seeking remain prevalent needs for many of their con-temporaries today.

But the liberation of any character for an actress seeking to play her begins with the text. So – what are we told about them at the opening of the play, and what did we discover? The first reference to them is made by Oliver and Charles the Wrestler in Act 1, Scene 1:

OLIVER   Can you tell if Rosalind, the Duke's daughter, be banish'd with her father?
CHARLES   O no; for the Duke's daughter, her cousin, so loves her, being ever from
    their cradles bred together, that she would have follow'd her exile, or have died to
    stay behind her. She is at the court, and no less belov'd of her uncle than his own
    daughter, and never two ladies lov'd as they do.   (lines 105–12)

Many questions are immediately thrown up – *was* it at Celia's insistence that Rosalind stayed behind? How old were the girls when the banishment took place? Was Celia old enough at the time to insist at all, given that later in the act she proclaims to her father that 'I did not then entreat to have her stay . . . I was too young that time to value her' (1.3.69–71)? What were Rosalind's feelings on the subject? Does Duke Frederick really love her as his own? If Rosalind was detained at Celia's insistence, does she have any feelings of resentment at having been deprived of her father as a consequence?

Several answers are provided as soon as they enter the play. Rosalind's opening words reveal a breach between her outer and inner selves – 'I *show* more mirth than I am mistress of' – and her words to Celia betray a certain severity. Celia's first words tell us a good deal too, and suggest fears for a certain imbalance in the relationship: 'Herein I see thou lov'st me not with the full weight that I love thee . . .' (1.2.8), etc. Celia goes on to assure Rosalind that she will restore, through her love, the losses inflicted on her friends by her father, and her speeches are full of terms of endearment. So we discover immediately that Rosalind is a divided spirit, part of her in exile with her father, and displaced; and that, for Celia, the wounds of the past lie between them, ever present, and can be healed only through the generosity of her affection. There is a sense of urgency about their respective declarations which suggests that the situation for them both is gathering momentum with time, not easing with it. The scene quickly changes gear, however, as Rosalind 'snaps out of it', and the two engage in an elaborate discussion about Fortune and Nature, revealing an ability to spark each other off through a shared facility with language and conceit that serves as an escape from their immediate surroundings.

We had a lot of difficulty with it in rehearsal (and performance!) because, presumably, somewhere along the line we have lost the capacity to chat conceptually. For Celia, the exchange seems more detached – the bandying of conceits and word-play – but Rosalind uses it to rationalise her own situation in a more personal way, accusing Dame Fortune of negligence in the distribution of 'her gifts to women'. We decided to clarify the story of the whole scene by placing it in a setting to which they have escaped – some kind of attic or nursery in which they can find refuge and thereby create, through word and thought, an imaginative world of their own. This took the form of an unused room, perhaps high up in the court, where Rosalind's father's abandoned belongings remain stacked and covered with dust-sheets. She might sneak off there in order to make some kind of contact with that other world for which she seems partially yearning. This design decision – which had far-reaching consequences – took root when discussions subsequently turned to what Arden was, and we evolved the idea that it was an imaginative realm rather than a version of Epping Forest – we decided as a company to explore the possibility that Arden could be created in such an attic, with dust-sheets twisting into trunks of trees and spreading like canopies of leaf, chests becoming tree-stumps, and so on. More of that anon. Back to the first scene and the discovery that the two girls have a facility for language which is both idiosyncratic and complementary; that it is the primary source of their shared sense of humour;

and that through their word-play they can escape – like many unhappy adolescents – to a world which is created by their pooled imaginations. All these discoveries are borne out as the play develops, and are crucial to the development of their relationship.

Two other facts spring off the page. The first is the dominant presence of their fathers, and the total absence of even a reference to their mothers, or indeed to any other women in the court (except Hisperia – the mole), laying emphasis on a world totally dominated by the male principle and its attendant values, a world in which we are shortly to see that the prevalent idea of a good time is to watch a wrestler bashing hell out of three young men and going for his fourth when he's killed them.

The second fact is that when Rosalind and Celia talk of devising 'sports', the former immediately suggests they talk about falling in love, betraying an interest in that state of mind, which is quickly and wittily punctured by Celia, who reveals less enthusiasm for the subject and even a certain distrust of it. Rosalind is clearly ripe with readiness for the experience – Celia is not.

Touchstone's arrival into the scene brings with it more information – their familiarity with him is obvious, and the speed with which he and Celia go into banter (only spasmodically joined by Rosalind) indicates both their mutual affection, and that Touchstone is, in part, privy to their private world. Celia's split loyalties and ambivalent feelings about her father are revealed clearly in the exchange, as she first sharply reprimands Touchstone's licence:

My father's love is enough to honour him: enough! Speak no more of him, you'll be whipt for taxation one of these days.

Then, in the next utterance:

By my troth, thou sayest true; for since the little wit that fools have was silenc'd, the little foolery that wise men have makes a great show.   (1.2.83–90)

This is more evidence that she, though in part her father's daughter, is clearly conscious of his repressive nature, and is taxed by the difficulty of reconciling the conflict. We noticed, too, how it is clearly Celia, throughout this section of the play, who leads and drives the scenes – the rhythms of her language are very indicative of a confident, even assertive, young woman, very rooted in her class, and at the centre of the court's 'culture'. Rosalind's speech-rhythms are markedly different, her thinking less linear and her utterances spasmodic, as though she were frequently only half-engaged. She also has the worst jokes, and after much struggling (to little avail!) some of them were cut as hopeless cases. We decided to pursue the idea that at this point in the play it is Celia who leads and initiates. We chose to disregard the need for Rosalind, as the play's 'heroine', to be the driving force until we reached a point when the text made it evident. Celia is more accessible, here, to the audience, as we discovered in performance, and Rosalind seems harder for them to get to know at this stage. It's the hardest area of the play for the actress playing her, because her silence must be placed by the production so that it has an eloquence – a problem we later discovered to be exactly paralleled by Celia in the second half of the play where Rosalind is well and truly in the driving seat. It is less the *form* of the speech around her that engages her, and more the *content* – when Le Beau enters to announce the wrestling, she seems half-heartedly to join in the teasing of him, but only really commits to the interchange when the subject turns to the fate of the three young off-stage wrestlers. Her immediate suggestion that they watch the ensuing match is a strange and telling one, as though she recognises something in the desperate youth who persists in going ahead with the fight, as though she hungers for experience, however brutal. She, too, has been wrestling, internally – her 'smoothness, her very silence and her patience' concealing an unexpressed rage and grief that somehow identify with the unknown youth.

This recognition, in time, became the clue to the speed with which Rosalind falls in love with Orlando. Falling in love at first sight presented us both with a problem, as actresses, because it seems so often to require the abandoning of one's own experience to some Elizabethan stage conven- tion. But, after a while, the solution seemed to lie in two important factors – readiness and recognition. That Rosalind is ready has already been discovered, and once Orlando enters (scantily clad, which helps!) and they are afforded the opportunity of dissuading him, he discloses a sense of isolation and despair which Rosalind seems to recognise. She ceases her suit immediately, and wishes him 'the little strength that I have' – a line of astonishing directness, familiarity, and even eroticism. If we see ourselves reflected in our lovers, then recognition must surely be the clue, and Orlando's subsequent unexpected triumph, against all odds, over Charles the champion must symbolise for Rosalind her own possibilities for conquest, and fuel the fire. That he then reveals himself to be the son of her own father's close friend confirms her rapid and passionate identification with him, and it is now that she begins to steer the scene and overtake a Celia bewildered by her friend's overt declarations and utter disregard for social convention. It's a glorious scene to play but one which took us a long time to get right, and pitch correctly, partly because it is tragic and comic and erotic all at once, but largely because everything is now happening at such speed. The wrestling match is crucially important to the first part of the play because of what it releases in all those attending it. Like paraffin thrown onto smouldering embers, it appears to ignite all those anarchic forces that have been lurking beneath the surface of social form, and within seconds (it seems to the actors) the lid springs off Duke Frederick's latest tyranny, Rosalind's passion, and Celia's grief at her father's wrongs. Orlando finds his heart in love and his life at stake.

In the midst of all this there is a short exchange between a Rosalind attempting to cohere her new feelings and a Celia trying to discover the extent and nature of them. Playing such an intimate scene between girlfriends, after the size and scale of what has just preceded it, was difficult at first. (It often is on those vast stages at Stratford and the Barbican, which lend themselves so easily to the public and spectacular but not easily to the private and confidential.) But looking more closely at the language of the scene gave us a clue as to the playing of it – the imagery is extreme, even violent. Verbs like 'throw', 'cast', 'lame', 'catch', 'shake', 'cry', 'try', 'wrestle', are used to express Rosalind's state, and love, instead of converting her melancholy into optimism and joy, seems rather to feed it. Their mutual enjoyment of word-play is still prevalent, but the two characters are already separating. For Celia, 'burrs' are thrown in 'holiday foolery', for Rosalind, they are 'in my heart'. It's a scene which we both found readily recognisable: the feeling of impending isolation that a girl experiences when her best friend's passions are diverted to the opposite sex and suddenly a gulf gapes between them.

But there is no time for actresses to wallow in this. In comes the Duke and within five lines Rosalind has been banished and a death sentence hangs over her head. Again, it all happens at an impossible speed, but interestingly the language now moves from prose to verse, providing us with a formality of structure with which to cohere the chaotic and attempt to rationalise the crisis. Rosalind's speech in self-defence is amazingly fluid and calm of rhythm, as though danger seems to lend her strength and clarity – information borne out by her later development as a character in Arden – and Celia, too, speaks out with a fluency and balance that matches her cousin's. For Celia, the scene is a watershed; she gives utterance to an accusation against Duke Frederick which, once released, seems to force her finally to resolve the divided loyalties between her friend and her father. The choice made, her passionate identification with Rosalind seems to have intensified to the point where she feels they are one:

CELIA   Prithee, be cheerful. Know'st thou not the Duke
        Hath banish'd me, his daughter?
ROSALIND   That he hath not.
CELIA   No, hath not? Rosalind lacks then the love
        Which teacheth thee that thou and I am one.   (1.3.94–7)

Her sentiments have both an adolescent ring of absolutism about them, and also an astonishingly mature consciousness of the power of love as an *educator* – a theme which is to be richly explored later in the play. Perhaps this is why we always found it difficult in rehearsal to pin the girls down to any particular age – an early decision to play them in their late teens turned out to be, at times, misleading, because of the sophistication and resonance of their thought, but it was always clear that their energies and preoccupations are youthful. In the end, we abandoned a firm decision on the matter, and allowed them to be older and younger as each scene demanded, a state which is generally typical, in any case, of young women poised between adolescence and adulthood. It became clearer to us in time that this is a crucial point in the play for Celia – her love for Rosalind seems to intensify because it has now become a sacrifice; there is cost and loss in it now, she has sunk everything into it, and the stakes are higher. Once again, we found the scene hard to play because of the speed with which they react, act, and make enormous decisions, but as ever the clue lies in *thought*. For a play which seems primarily to be about *feelings*, it in fact allows the actors little space to indulge in these, for the drive forward springs constantly from the *thinking* which propels the action ever onward and outward, and requires considerable discipline in the playing.

This scene, the concluding one for Rosalind and Celia at court, contains more fundamental clues. It's interesting to note that no sooner has Celia rejected her own father, than she proposes they go off in search of another – Rosalind's. Their world is still constructed around figures of paternal authority. It's also interesting to notice their rather fantastical and contradictory ideas about what Arden will be – a forest full of predatory thieves and assailants (like the forests of our fears and dreams) but also clearly a place where 'our jewels and our wealth' are going to be of some practical use – when the 'curtle-axe' and 'boar-spear' fail them, perhaps? Fiona's decision to root Celia's class in the world of Sloane Square paid dividends here – clearly, like all young creatures from her privileged background, Celia believes that money can buy you anything, even in the desert. But perhaps the most important key to their story in this scene lies in the fact that it is still Celia who initiates the ideas – of flight, of Arden, of seeking Duke Senior, of their practical requirements, and of disguise. It's the idea that they transform themselves into other people that first *really* engages Rosalind's imagination, and the speed with which she picks it up and develops the cross-dressing idea seems to lend her a confidence and courage which thereafter will never leave her – it is the first real initiative that she has taken in the play so far, and it speaks volumes that it is *this* that releases her imagination and contacts her positive, forward-looking energies. Interesting, too, that it's a warrior-man that she conceives for her disguise, a fighting figure with obvious resonances in relation to Orlando, though not without witty observation of the absurdity of manly bravado. The energy, as experienced in the playing, now flies between them as they finalise the details and head, no longer for 'danger' and thieves, but for *liberty*. Finally, it's perhaps the only point in the play at which they are completely equal – both disinherited now, both fatherless, neither of them any longer with anything to lose and equally matched in their confidence, daring, exhilaration, and mutual interdependence. It has never been the case up till now, and it may never be again.

And so to Arden. The nature of this place was the source of constant debate throughout the rehearsal and performance of our production. Adrian Noble and the designer Bob Crowley had made an early choice which we were fully in support of – to reject the traditional conception of Arden as a kind of theatrical arcadia reminiscent of Suffolk, full of logs and boughs and rivers of trout, where the inhabitants slap their thighs, jump off stumps and wear feathered caps at a jaunty angle. The play is so clearly *not* a rural romp, and Shakespeare's description of the forest bears no relation to the familiar or recognisable – it is a 'desert' and 'uncouth', it is referred to as bleak and barren, but also as containing lionesses and snakes like a jungle or plain; it seems to be a strange, weird realm which has the power to transform itself, and in which all things are possible. It is both an image from our nightmares and a place of infinite potential. Above all, we felt, it is a metaphor. But a metaphor for *what* exactly? We all shared a desire to jolt the audience out of their rustic expectations, but to make coherent the metaphor which replaces those became the production's most difficult challenge to itself. If it is a realm of the imagination, then of *whose* imagination? Who, then, are the natives, like Corin, Silvius, Phoebe, and Audrey? Figments of this imagination? Exiles from the town? Not Corin and Audrey, surely. A thousand questions beg to be asked, but perhaps they do not all – *cannot* all – require a coherent and unified answer. In Stratford the Arden set directly reflected the court set of the first half: but sombre blacks turned to green, clocks lost their faces, and mirrors their reflective glass. The vast sheet of white silk that first covered the ground as a snowscape was lifted, with the arrival of spring, and hung from the flies loosely in a tree-shape – but with possibilities for transformation into a hiding-place, a wedding-canopy or anything else that the scenes required of it. The problem evolved, however, that it both occupied too much space and prominence, and seemed to become excessively metaphorical – in the end, we discovered, one cannot *act* with a metaphor, and the inhabitants of Arden must be allowed space and light. So when the production transferred to London it was simplified, the silk taking a less obtrusive position upstage, and more successfully affording a cleaner, clearer environment for Arden's expansive terrain.

Into this terrain, in midwinter, Celia and Rosalind arrive, a miserable Touchstone in tow. In terms of the girls' story, the scene seems to serve two functions. First it strips them of their rather mythical preoccupations about Arden and brings them harshly face to face with the realities of exhaustion, cold, and hunger. Perhaps such a stripping process is necessary if two young women from sheltered and privileged origins are to make the leap successfully into their new lives – obsessions with fathers, the past, old guilt, and new love may disintegrate if you haven't eaten for three days – and in this way they must experience hardship in order to re-emerge. The second function of the scene is to explore how their relationship is changed by Rosalind's new male identity. At the outset, none of them are coping well, but Rosalind's new garb defines a role for her as comforter of the 'weaker vessel', and, as always with her, strength is derived from role-play, from identification with something other, so that by the end of the scene she has passed the first test, discovered that as a man she can become both a property-owner and an employer, and has clearly replaced Celia as the 'doer' of the two. Celia remains, hilariously, herself – ever preferring discussion of food to discussions of love, and rather cavalierly promising to 'mend' Corin's 'wages', in true Sloane-style, as she picks up her spirits and her luggage and heads off to the sheepcote. We found that this opens up an important area of choice about Celia: whereas Rosalind continues to transform herself and experiment with identity and role-play right to the end, Celia seems to retain her original 'self-ness'. Her language rhythms remain rooted in her class and it's debatable whether she ever achieves the common touch – or even aspires to it.

This is not to say Celia is not happy. The next scene between them (Act 3, Scene 2) was an endless delight to play, as Spring arrives in the forest along with Orlando's absurdly derivative love-poems, affording Celia full rein for her customary amusement at the absurdity of it all, while Rosalind, who initially shares the laugh, turns on a sixpence and becomes wonderingly curious, ridiculously flattered, and vastly available for teasing. Their mutual relish of language and complementary wit remain at the heart of the scene, despite the differences in their respective states. Orlando's arrival changes the gear, however, and from this point the play moves forward into new territory: we will never again see them so at ease with one another.

The arrival of her beloved transforms Rosalind yet again. From the second in which she informs a bewildered Celia that she will 'speak to him like a saucy lackey', she moves into the fast lane, never to return. She is

9   Rosalind and Celia in the Forest of Arden

released once again by a new identity, and driven by a tireless energy that draws its source from the anarchic power of sexual love, a power further fuelled, as the scene develops, by its reciprocation in the wrestling Orlando. Her life's experience as an observer transforms her first into a witty social satirist, parodying ignorant priests and lazy lawyers in a dazzling improvised display to grab Orlando's attention; then into a knowledgeable native inventing her own history (and Celia's) off the top of her head; then into a detached expert on matters of love; and finally into Orlando's own counsellor as the idea of the game emerges at the peak of the scene. It was always a monumental challenge for Rosalind, this scene. The actress playing her requires an alacrity of thought and nimbleness of tongue second to none, as Rosalind's language dances out of her spirit in ever-lengthening arcs of prose, allowing barely a chance to breathe. Reaction must be channelled immediately into action, and she quite literally seems to leave the ground.

For the actress playing Celia – at least in our experience – the major challenge of the second half of the play emerges: that of Celia's silence. As Rosalind becomes increasingly in possession of her powers, Celia is left powerless, drawn into a game which is not of her making, and dazzled by a friend who is now barely recognisable. Rosalind, discovering as Ganymede the ecstatic freedom of invention and fantasy, creates a world in which she can engage with Orlando in the utmost intimacy, without actually yielding herself up to him – but is this a world which includes Celia? Celia is obliged to listen impassively. She finds herself cast in the role of the shepherdess sister, her father transformed into 'an old religious uncle . . . who was in his youth an inland man'. She hears her own gender spectacularly slandered and finally witnesses the establishment of Orlando's prospective 'love-cure', which clearly implies that she may find herself obliged to sit through such ordeals *daily*. The options available to us both, in the scene that starts all this, were numerous.

What *is* Celia's attitude to it all? Wonder, horror, amusement, rage, confusion, isolation, jubilation, fear, or all of these? How should she be placed physically on the set? Should she be at the side, like a spectator, or centrally, as a third character in the action? Does Rosalind need her there, drawing on her presence to take ever-increasing risks, or does she quite literally forget her until the last line of the scene ('Come, sister, will you go?')? Does Celia exit with the 'lovers' or make her own way off to strike out for independence? We experimented a good deal over the course of the run, and our final decisions included many of the options at once. It seemed increasingly certain that Rosalind draws strongly on Celia's presence; to show off, outrage, seek refuge in, and silently confer with – as it is often possible to be braver with your best friend at hand, and as the presence of an observer frequently does afford greater freedom, rather than less. Most importantly, perhaps, Rosalind might not be able to trust herself if left alone with Orlando, so that Celia, whether she likes it or not, becomes a kind of chaperone-cum-referee. If we argued at all (actresses playing these parts are *supposed* to fight furiously, but in truth we only came to blows a handful of times!) it was over the question of rhythm. Rosalind's text is almost a musical score and its pulse is insistent, fast, and precise, so to break it seemed to be to let the energies of the scene drop irrevocably onto the floor. Celia, on the other hand, has none, and so her opportunities for contributing to the scene must depend on non-verbal intervention and situational rather than linguistic humour. In the end, the problem is partly resolved by the fourth player – the audience – whose response to the scene and its glorious revelations inevitably serves to punctuate and shape it.

So Rosalind exits in triumph, to re-enter shortly afterwards in desolation, accompanied by a Celia temporarily restored to her position as mistress of the situation:

ROSALIND   Never talk to me, I will weep.
CELIA   Do, I prithee, but yet have the grace to consider that tears do not become
a man . . .   (3.4.1–3)

For some reason we found this scene hugely problematical in the playing. From reading it, it is hard to see why. It seems to be a minutely observed, deliciously funny little scene which should have the audience in stitches of amusement and recognition. It didn't. Not a titter. We tried everything on it – we ate bananas, fished, lay on our backs, sat side by side, stood on opposite sides – manifold attempts to establish that sense of *situation* which we hoped would liberate the comedy. And how to pitch it? If Rosalind's tears are literal and plentiful then Celia emerges as faintly sadistic. If they are not, a danger emerges in Rosalind seeming to be striking hollow attitudes. And who is leading whom? Is Rosalind's fervour the scene's driving force, or is Celia indulging a certain smugness and manipulating the entire exchange? For the last months of the run, it finally resolved itself, almost of its own accord. The scene became tender and true and funny: perhaps because we had ceased to force it in any way; perhaps because by then we were so sure who we were as characters that the audience could enjoy the same relaxation; but perhaps most importantly because the scene, like a microcosm of the whole play, proved itself to be beyond definitions like 'comic' or 'tragic' and once we had abandoned preconceptions and trusted its rhythms, accuracy, and innate wit, it rewarded us.

In terms of the women's relationship, there were clues to be found in the fact that Rosalind is no longer picking up on Celia's wit and word-play – Celia's irony is met now by the most urgent and earnest of responses, as Rosalind experiences the agony and vulnerability of the lover while Celia, uninvolved and therefore in full possession of herself, resorts to undercutting and may even be in danger of exploiting the situation. The choices available, once again, were numerous. Are Celia's remarks about Orlando for her own amusement, a vested interest, the expression of frustration, or possibly a genuine attempt to remove the scales from her companion's eyes? It's also interesting to note that for two girls previously so obsessed with fathers in general and seeking Duke Senior in particular, only the most casual of passing references to him is made by Rosalind, as a piece of old news she's forgotten to pass on:

I met the Duke yesterday, and had much question with him. He ask'd me of what parentage I was. I told him of as good as he, so he laugh'd and *let me go*. But what talk we of fathers, when there is such a man as Orlando? (3.4.35–9; our italics)

For Rosalind fathers have been replaced by lovers and by a growing sense of her own, autonomous identity. For Celia, with neither father nor lover, but only a friend from whom she is increasingly separated by experience, this may be a moment of enormous vulnerability.

The arrival of Silvius and Phoebe into the scene sees a radical gear-change, and a further development in Rosalind's transformation. Once again, another identity lends her daring and freedom, and as a 'busy actor' she steps into the arena with confidence restored and in full flight – a zealot, now, in matters of love. Her sense of outrage at Phoebe's treatment of Silvius is genuine and impassioned, but also wickedly funny, and once again Celia acts as spectator – but with less personally at stake than in the scenes with Orlando. We felt confident that her silence on this occasion can be interpreted as an appreciative one, and that the advent of Phoebe's infatuation with Ganymede would lead Celia to exit with Rosalind, the two united again in convulsions of laughter at the absurdity of the situation.

From this point in the play – Act 3, Scene 5 – until its closing stages it becomes very difficult to chart the course of this friendship. Rosalind is now so launched on her own voyage, and her quest to experience, challenge, and explore not only her own passions and possibilities but those of everyone else she encounters lends her a vision and a zeal which appear to leave Celia far behind. If love is an education, then hers is now informing her with insight, wisdom, and a capacity to measure the inner person, as illustrated in her scene with Jaques (the beginning of Act 4, Scene 1) which leads her into a territory whose horizons seem way beyond Celia's reach. In the second long wooing scene with Orlando which follows, Rosalind develops at astonishing speed, now completely *reversing* the traditional gender roles of man as teacher, woman as pupil. As Ganymede she can gain further access to Orlando's heart and mind by talking 'man to man', and it's interesting how her wit now enters the world of male humour in the exchange about snails, horns, and cuckoldry. By 'acting out' Rosalind, she can explore her own horizons, free to articulate her own doubts and fears, and to discover and challenge all Orlando's preconceptions and resistances on the subject of women, sexuality, and marriage. As the imagery of her language grows hidden and more anarchic, she probes even further, pushing him to limits so dangerous that it seems he is brought to a point where he is forced to extract himself from the scene, and departs: 'For these two hours, Rosalind, I will leave thee' (4.1.177).

Celia, who at the scene's outset seems to have settled for her role as referee and 'priest', is soon silenced by its dangerous developments, but it is now a less ambivalent silence for the actress playing her – when Orlando leaves, there is an exchange between the two women which leaves us in little doubt as to the gulf that now divides them. Celia bitterly chastises her friend for having 'misused our sex in your love-prate', but Rosalind is lost to her, reeling at the discovery of her passion's boundless horizons, and unable to exist now 'out of the sight of Orlando'. Lines between reality and fantasy have now merged and evaporated for her, and the fact that she calls Celia 'Aliena' seems to set the seal on their divide. Love has the capacity to make people both enormously generous and utterly selfish, and it seemed to us that Rosalind has now abandoned all sensibility in relation to her cousin, and Celia is alone.

It's at this point that Shakespeare brings Oliver in. The speed with which Celia falls in love with him may be the same speed with which Rosalind recognises and falls in love with Orlando, but after a while we felt it to be a different choice – one informed by a realisation of Rosalind's emotional absence. If our loves are informed to a great extent by our situations, then Celia is now available, and readiness is all. Oliver is a new man, and his eloquent account of his transformation takes Celia through his 'rebirth' again, so that their meeting is informed by knowledge and truth. Celia's last line in the scene – 'Good sir, go with us' – is her last in the play, and the two women never speak to each other again.

It need not be the silence now of separation. From this point until the end, the play becomes another beast, a creature of new dimensions into which each character's separate through-line or private experience is absorbed. Rosalind, ever-changing, becomes a sort of ring-mistress, drawing together all the threads in the play; a kind of conjuror, creating a collective ritual out of the chaos, and rewarding faith with mysterious revelation. She is now both man and woman, in a way, and as such can transcend reality to become a creature of magic who brings a god to her wedding. But if the play has moved onto another plane now, the last act remains problematical for actresses. That Rosalind chooses to make her final entrance not alone, but with Celia, gave us a welcome opportunity to make contact with each other again, and afforded us a brief moment to resolve the journey the two women have travelled together. But the fact remains that in the play's closing moments it is Duke Senior who resumes charge, and traditional values seem in danger of being celebrated. This, at the end of a play which so fully and radically explores the complexities of sexuality, maleness, and femaleness, and sends gender boundaries flying, was endlessly difficult to play. In Stratford, we came to feel that the production was somehow at risk in washing over those difficulties, and that we were required to become different people in those last moments. In London we re-staged the ending quite radically, and the problem was eased.

In Stratford Hymen had been represented as a flickering silhouette on a lighted screen, placed upstage, obliging the actors to turn away from the audience to perceive him – this both threw the focus onto an unlikely manifestation which threatened the audience's capacity to believe in what was going on, and deprived them of the characters' responses to the deity and his dictates. In London, Hymen became a mere beam of light whose source was *behind* the audience, so that the actors beheld him facing out front. In this way, the audience was able to focus not on the god, but on the faces of those whose futures he is deciding. This afforded each of us the opportunity to play against the 'happy ever after' element, if we chose.

The dance, too, was changed. In Stratford it was rather formal, and had been in slight danger of ritualising the segregation of the sexes – and it was unchallenging to the complexity of the coupling. In London it was altered, becoming a more informal and spontaneous expression, in a folk tradition:

a collective celebration of the fact that what was sought had been found; a coming together. In Stratford the dance had lulled the play to its close, and the dancers remained on stage for Rosalind's address to the audience. We came to realise that this created problems for the audience, who did not know whether the characters were staying in Arden or not, or *who*, exactly, was talking to them in the epilogue. In London, the dance culminated in a moment of still suspension, as the characters took in the Arden they were about to leave, and absorbed the *consequences* of the return to the ordered world. They then exited, through a moon-shaped hole in the backdrop, which both told the story more clearly and laid emphasis on the fantastical nature of the whole event. With Rosalind alone on stage, the epilogue then clearly became a separate event, allowing the questions thrown up by the play's finale to be left in the air.

These changes meant that the issues explored were no longer smothered, at the end, by excesses of 'merry-making', and we no longer felt obliged to abandon ourselves on the stage to some imposed inevitability. After much working and re-working the complexity of the play's resolution was *taken on*.

Indeed, working and re-working became the hallmark of our experience in this production. Like Rosalind and Celia, what we encountered was a journey – from the first day's rehearsal in January 1985 to the closing performance in London some eighteen months later, we never stopped working on it, chipping away, seeking new developments, encountering our resistances and trying to battle with them, changing choices and experimenting. Both of us found it a play of wondrous delights but formidable complexity, but we were lucky that the production gave us, finally, the space in which to draw upon our own experience, our own humour, and our own lunacies, passions, and sensibilities – and, primarily, upon our own friendship. If the struggle for women is a struggle to be human in a world which declares them only to be female, then this was the territory of *As You Like It* which most engaged and challenged us. If we even in part gave resonance to the story of Rosalind and Celia, then the struggle was richly rewarded.

Jaques in
As You Like It

ALAN RICKMAN

ALAN RICKMAN played Jaques in Adrian Noble's production of *As You Like It* at Stratford in 1985 and at the Barbican in the following year. Other roles that season were Achilles in *Troilus and Cressida* and the Vicomte de Valmont in *Les Liaisons Dangereuses*, which he later played in the West End and in New York. At the Barbican in 1986 he also played Hendrik Höfgen in *Mephisto*. He first appeared with the RSC in 1978 when his roles included Ferdinand in *The Tempest* and Boyet in *Love's Labour's Lost*. Among his earlier work were performances at the Edinburgh Festival and at the National Theatre in *Measure for Measure* and Ben Jonson's *The Devil is an Ass*. His television roles include that of Mr Slope in *The Barchester Chronicles*.

You can dress *As You Like It* in any clothes, jump up and down on tree stumps or slip and slide on white silk as we did, but it goes into a big sulk if you don't remain open to what has always been sitting there on the page. What that *is* will change its resonance from production to production but more as a result of the particular individuals playing the roles than of directorial schemes.

That is not meant to be actors' megalomania. I say it with some confidence, however, because over the eighteen months that we played it the production's emphasis did shift from a concern for staging effects towards making its characters' inner lives more visible. By the time it closed in London there was hardly a moment which hadn't been simplified so that the play could breathe more easily. Maybe that process should have been in operation earlier, but it is true to say that it could have continued indefinitely – no one felt we had ever 'arrived', there was always a desire to keep the production alive and changing, and it was good to know that predominant among its devoted fans were school parties to whom Shakespeare had previously meant exams and boredom. I feel very protective towards Jaques, the play, and the production in all their elusiveness. I have a love–hate relationship with white silk.

10   Alan Rickman as Jaques, 1985

What follows is *my* version of the thoughts and decisions made between Adrian Noble, the other actors and myself which resulted in *this* Jaques in *this* production of *As You Like It*. None of it should be confused with fact; it is a piece of total bias.

Before rehearsals began, I knew that for many people Jaques is either their favourite or least favourite Shakespearean character, that he carries with him a reputation for having his arms permanently folded and eyebrows forever arched, and that he's the one who does 'All the world's a stage'. I had played the part once before, eight years previously, so I was already sure that he was more than a famous speech on legs. However, as we worked, I found an even clearer picture of a Jaques who is perceptive but passionate, vulnerable but anarchic, and a man whose means of expressing these qualities was completely unpredictable. He's very sure of himself and a bit of a mess.

There was certainly room to explore all that in rehearsals, and the production did ask us to lay ourselves on the line, but I wanted to keep a sense of Jaques the improviser – a jack-in-the-box quality of what's he up to? Who's he getting at? – particularly with the Duke and the lords. In fact, writing this I'm not sure how conscious a decision it was – mostly the memories are of missing the boat; the other actors must have tired of wondering where I was going to enter from next, or if there would ever be a recognisable shape to the scene, but we created an air of mutual surprise to work in which seemed profitable, and it was born out of what I saw as evidence on the page.

What is Jaques's story? Was he one of the three or four loving lords described by Charles as having initially followed the Duke into exile, or is he one of the merry men who turned up later to live like old Robin Hood of England and to fleet the time carelessly?

Jaques does not deny the Duke's accusation that he has been 'a libertine', he calls the court 'pompous', and his lyrics to Amiens's song speak for themselves.

> If it do come to pass,
> That any man turn ass,
> Leaving his wealth and ease
> A stubborn will to please,
> Ducdame, ducdame, ducdame!
> Here shall he see
> Gross fools as he,
> And if he will come to me. (2.5.50–7)

This, after we have heard the Duke's attempt to raise morale among the freezing troops by suggesting that they kill some venison, coupled with the story of Jaques crying over a dead deer. Does this add up to a picture of harmony in the woodland glades? Before Jaques has even appeared the image I receive of him from the lord's story is already one of antagonism, compassion, and energy. Nor is the Duke's response one of concern for Jaques, but an immediate desire to find him.

> I love to cope him in these sullen fits,
> For then he's full of matter. (2.1.67–8)

Jaques the entertainer, the radical, someone to wind up. Good value.

I think Jaques is in the forest because it's a less boring option than Duke Frederick's court (where he would surely have been certified) and because, ex-devil that he is, he still needs the odd brick wall to bang his head against. Jaques seeks, ferrets, prods, and interferes but he doesn't *do*. His self-sufficiency is shaky at the best of times, but he definitely needs the other lords to cook his food.

Taking a few liberties with the order in which these lines appear in the play, here's how Jaques describes himself.

I can suck melancholy out of a song, as a weasel sucks eggs. It is a melancholy of mine own, compounded of many simples, extracted from many objects, and indeed the sundry contemplation of my travels, in which my often rumination wraps me in a most humorous sadness. O that I were a fool! I am ambitious for a motley coat. It is my only suit. I must have liberty withal, as large a charter as the wind, to blow on whom I please, for so fools have. Give me leave to speak my mind and I will through and through cleanse the foul body of th'infected world, if they will patiently receive my medicine. What, for a counter, would I do but good? Tis good to be sad and say nothing. So to your pleasures, I am for other than for dancing measures. To see no pastime I. I have gain'd my experience. God buy you, and you talk in blank verse.

The first new acquaintance Jaques makes in the forest is Touchstone, who of course wouldn't dream of addressing anyone in blank verse, and when Jaques runs back to the lords like a child with a new toy and starts on 'A fool, a fool! I met a fool i'th'forest . . .' it is at once a description, a flight of fancy, and an idealisation. The improvisatory quality is at its height, and this is Jaques flying, but he is also at his most vulnerable and wide open for attack. 'What for a counter would I do but good?', he says, and I always thought this was the most naked view of Jaques that we are given. A simple line that is immediately punished by the Duke's knowledge of Jaques's past. It is as if Jaques is saying 'Let me be a fool, let me say what I think and I'll cure the world.' 'You?' says the Duke, 'You're diseased. They'll all catch it.'

The best way to rattle Jaques is to interrupt or alter his rhythm in this way. The 'Who cries out on pride' speech which follows is notoriously difficult, and in early rehearsals I would cling to the sense for dear life. The effect of this, of course, was to make it more dense than ever, and it wasn't until I put all its disjointedness and seeming non-sequiturs into the mouth of a wounded and trapped animal that the speech had any real focus in the scene. Or in other words, put rhythm and sense together and you find that yet again Shakespeare has done the work for you.

This also opened up what looked like a more accurate route into 'All the world's a stage.' Orlando's entrance, his hunger and his concern for Adam, elicits a massive platitude from the Duke. 'This wide and universal theatre . . .' (etc., etc.). Jaques has had time to gather his resources and is ready to pounce. 'All the world's a stage' starts on a half-line so it is an immediate reply. He has been provoked into it by what he sees as the leaden sensibilities around him – 'There then! how then? what then?' – but in a

11 'Forbear, and eat no more – why, I have eat none yet'
Orlando (Hilton Macrae) interrupts the Duke's banquet

way it is also an example of Jaques as his own worst enemy. It is a speech of indelible imagery, shot through with savage apparent-truths, but it is the speech of an extremist. Seven ages, not one with a glimmer of hope. Of course, he's wrong. After 'Sans teeth, sans eyes, sans taste, sans every thing', Adam is brought on exhausted but not senile – the essence of courage and loyalty.

Bearing all this in mind, I could never see a measured trip through life as a real possibility. In fact, I thought there should be occasions during the speech when Jaques might be in real danger of losing control. And it is impossible to be unaware that you are delivering one of the most famous speeches in literature. 'Mount Everest? . . . Where?'

If, as Beerbohm writes, *As You Like It* is not a play but an extended lyric, then 'All the world's a stage' is one of its great arias. That's what I went for anyway, trying also to keep its roots tethered in the scene. Hang on to it and let it go at the same time. A suitably impossible aim. It was also used as a kind of fulcrum to the production since the interval was taken at the end of that scene. The play moved from Winter to Spring, and the design from white to green. The second half was always a more relaxed experience for me. If 'All the world's a stage' shows Jaques cursed by his own perception, the second half shows the result – condemned to wander forever, endlessly trying to relocate some innocence, endlessly disappointed. And it is Jaques who initiates the conversations with Touchstone, Orlando, and Rosalind, and Jaques who, when disarmed, runs away. Therein lie both his vulnerability and his arrogance.

There is another irony, too. He is also able to function as an occasional breeze to an audience who might otherwise become too heady on Rosalind and Orlando, because of course he doesn't change. He starts the play offstage under a tree by a stream, and ends it offstage sitting in a cave. He hasn't gone off to look for the convertite Duke – Duke Senior says 'Stay, Jaques, stay', and this he happily misinterprets as meaning the Duke has things to discuss. This is the Duke of whom Jaques says, 'I think of as many matters as he, but I give heaven thanks, and make no boast of them' (2.5.35-7). This is the Duke who, at the end, seems to have learned little from Arden – 'Now you had three acres, and he had seventeen, and I had three hundred and eighty-four . . .' What would they have to talk about? I think Jaques is just running on the spot.

So you are left with an image of complete aloneness, mirrored, incidentally, by the fact that the actor walks into the wings and twiddles his thumbs while everyone else is dancing. And in some ways it is a lonely part to play; Jaques starts each scene with his ears pricked and ends them with his tail between his legs. But a curious complicity is established with the audience which allows a lot of warmth in. They frequently seem to share the same set of eyes, and idiosyncratic though it may be, I think he's got a great sense of humour:

> And I did laugh sans intermission
> An hour by his dial.

As I have already mentioned, I played Jaques once before. This was in a production by Peter James at the Crucible Theatre, Sheffield, and I think that is where those seeds were sown. The production was certainly not flippant but Peter has never been averse to a cheap gag, and that was as joyous an experience as this one was complex. It was in modern dress, played in the round (famous speeches have to be done revolving slowly on the spot) and on an abstract set – a huge roof of white strips of cloth which could be called down to conceal anyone who needed to hide. I have vivid memories of Audrey, Touchstone, and William singing 'Shake it up Shakespeare baby', while eleven hundred people rocked with laughter, and it never seemed even remotely an error of taste. That's how tolerant the play can be. It was a production rooted in a corporate joy. This one seemed to place its characters at a succession of crossroads in order to watch their individual choices. Indeed, Jaques this time round was quite literally older and wiser, but given that first instincts should be guarded jealously, those early discoveries were invaluable.

After one of our last performances, knowing that I was to contribute to this book, I wrote this:

Today we have performed *As You Like It* twice, and tiredness sometimes brings a freedom which lets you know how much the 'work' has been pushed into the background and the character just behaves. There are discoveries I only really make in performance. He is a bit unco-ordinated, given to darting about or standing very still, finding imaginary itches, restless and nervy, not comfortable ever. Periods of great concentration and others when easily distracted. Full of private smiles.

That day, I was also to be visited by the ex-head of the English department at my old school. He had sent a card saying 'How are you getting on with Jaques? I always thought he was an old bore.' He was coming to my dressing-room at the same time as a young 'A' level student who wanted me to answer questions for her theatre-studies project. 'Did I see Jaques as anything more than a self-indulgent cynic?'

There must be fifty years between those two questions but Jaques seems to have been imprisoned by teachers', pupils' and audiences' preconceptions as much as by those of Duke Senior.

I just wanted to let him out.

Viola in
Twelfth Night

ZOË WANAMAKER

Z OË WANAMAKER played Viola in John Caird's production of *Twelfth Night* at Stratford in 1983 and at the Barbican the following year. In the same season (her second with the RSC) she played Adriana in *The Comedy of Errors* and Kitty Duval in Saroyan's *The Time of Your Life*. She first came to Stratford in 1978 to play Bianca in *The Taming of the Shrew*, Gemma Beech in *Captain Swing*, and Toine in *Piaf*, the last transferring to the West End and later to New York. Earlier Shakespearean work had included Katherina in *The Taming of the Shrew*, Hermia in *A Midsummer Night's Dream*, and another version of Viola. Among numerous other stage roles have been Sally Bowles in *Cabaret*, Eliza in *Pygmalion*, Stella in *A Streetcar Named Desire*, and (for the RSC) May Daniels in *Once in a Lifetime* and Kattrin in *Mother Courage*. Her film work includes *Inside the Third Reich* and *The Hunger* and on television she has appeared in numerous programmes including *Spy Trap*, *Danton's Death*, *Baal*, *Enemies of the State*, and *All the World's a Stage*.

I had played Viola some ten years before John Caird's Stratford production of *Twelfth Night*, in a version directed by Richard Cotterill for the Cambridge Theatre Company. The sense (the constant sense in doing Shakespeare) that that version had not come up to expectations left me, however, quite ready to accept a second invitation to attempt the part. I had been in the Stratford company only once before, in 1978, mainly to play in new work at The Other Place (*Piaf* and *Captain Swing*) though I had been on the main stage as Bianca in Michael Bogdanov's production of *The Taming of the Shrew*. Now I was back, dauntingly, for two major Shakespearean roles, Adriana in *The Comedy of Errors*, and Viola.

To undertake a major role at Stratford is to be haunted by the past. As you go into the Royal Shakespeare Theatre you are faced with twelve-foot high pictures of other actors who have done other performances of your part, and their history and their triumphs loom over you: 'Follow that!' It's like coming to Mecca; the ghosts are all around and the fear of failure is very great. Having been brought up through the sixties when new work by new writers was the prime objective in my kind of theatre, the thought of speaking Shakespeare's verse on the Stratford stage was inevitably frightening.

This sense of insecurity remained when the production opened. Was I speaking the text as it should be spoken, was I being true to it, to the production, to the character? After a year in Stratford, a year of struggle to be relaxed in the role and yet to keep it fresh, we moved to London, to the Barbican, where, with some modifications to the set and alterations to Viola's costume (and some cast changes too, including a new Olivia and a new Sir Toby), and some new ideas that I had been mulling over during the break, I found myself much more confident in the words and began to enjoy myself in the part. Confidence in the text as a springboard, an innate sense of not having to think about the words or about saying them right, these things allowed the play to become a conversation in which I was at home, to become organic. But a year to find that sense is a long time.

12   Zoë Wanamaker as Viola with Orsino (Miles Anderson), 1983

The basic aim of John Caird's production was to focus on the pain of love. *Twelfth Night* deals with many kinds of love: Viola's, the most pure, constant as the sea is constant, the sea that gives her her life, and her brother his, and her brother back to her; Malvolio's love, self-deluding, ultimately self-centred; Olivia's love of mourning, for her father and, reflecting Viola, for her brother; Orsino's adoring love, which puts woman on a pedestal; Antonio's faithful, painful love of Sebastian; Maria's dogged love of Sir Toby; Sir Toby's love of wasting time; each character disguising the truth about himself and from himself. The play is a fairly simple one, really, a story about time, about growing up and growing old. It has the concentrated quality of a chamber piece, and its form is a complete circle, a point we tried to mark in our production, which began with the sounds of storm and rain and ended with Feste singing of them as these sounds returned. Illyria seems to be a place that is frozen in time, where the social order is locked, where self-delusion, disguise, and hierarchy create an impasse for the people who live with them. And then Viola arrives and her presence disturbs everyone and moves the play through chaos and at last into seeming harmony but with that last strange coda of Feste's song, and Malvolio still locked in self-delusion, disguised even to himself. The catalyst, the driving force of the play is Viola; and the responsibility of that was on me.

To have played the part before was not helpful, not relevant. I wanted to come to it as a blank sheet of paper, to let it sit in my head while I was reading it, reading it once and just trying to find where my instincts were on that first reading, what my first impressions of the play were, trying to wipe out the old tunes of the way I had done it before. Much of that early reading, too, was for the sounds, the rhythms, the movement of the iambic line, which to me is not instinctive but something I have to work at, a secret code to be penetrated, like music; but for this text, certainly, a wonderful route to the deeper flow of the play – and, indeed, to the simple process of learning the words, which for me (touched with dyslexia) is not an easy process at all. In these early stages I was looking for all the clues I could find about what kind of person Viola is, what other characters say about her, what would happen to the story of the play if she were taken away, but always concentrating on the actual structure of her text, the precise choice of words. I also did a little research into the twin syndrome, though time, and the sense that Shakespeare's insistence on brother and sister twins being indistinguishable means that he is not thinking very realistically, left this avenue only partially explored. Rehearsals were, as ever, a tough and arduous search, a fumbling with the labyrinthine twists and turns of the script, a slow process of getting to know the other actors and their ideas, their interpretations of their roles; of argument and discussion and trying to fit it all in and to make the story of these people understandable and the play's ideas, wonderful and extraordinary, clear to an audience.

Eventually we got onto the set, designed by Robin Don and lit by David Hersey, a rocky landscape next to the sea, dominated by a tree, an autumnal-looking tree, its branches fanning out like a sea coral, above and beyond the proscenium arch. Costumes too were autumnal, in rusts and browns and olives, and traditionally Elizabethan. From the auditorium it was, I'm told, a very beautiful set, but for us, as we discovered at the technical rehearsals, there were huge problems, particularly with the terrain. The tree, and the rocky inclines, left an acting area only a few feet across, and though there was some levelling following the technical rehearsals, difficulties remained throughout the Stratford season. The set was partly supposed to represent a sort of nightmare, and the lighting was subdued to give an atmosphere of emotional turmoil, discovery of self, growing up, but the translation of these concepts into practical stage terms was not without difficulties for us. It was hard to find your light, and the unevenness of the floor was exacerbated by the eight-inch wide trough for the safety iron, in which many an ankle was in peril of being turned during the season; getting down from the top of the rocks at the back was hazardous; and the tree, which had looked so delicate on the model, the little veins of the coral like a lovely leaf-skeleton, had to be made much more substantial because of the need to dismantle it so often during the season for changes of play in the Stratford repertoire system. All these things were part of the disappointment (not unusual) of turning initial concepts and ideas into concrete, and sometimes cumbersome, reality. At the Barbican I think the set worked better, partly, no doubt, because we were more used to it, but also because the wider stage allowed more room on either side of it, and there was some more levelling out, and altered lighting. In London I was much happier, too, with my costume, which had been such a disappointment when I first wore it at the Stratford technical rehearsal. The thick corduroy trousers and waistcoat, which to me had always seemed lumpy, were changed to a light suede and I found myself much more relaxed and easy, able to use the pockets. I felt much more like a boy in it, and the sense of greater ease was increased by cutting my own hair very short and so discarding the wig which had always bothered me. Audiences, I think, enjoyed the literal quality of the set, the tree, the rocks, and the thunderstorm, and the music by Ilona Sekacz, beautiful and magical, and the sound of the sea which was ever present, the giver and taker of life, dark and threatening yet at the same time mysterious and romantic.

The young woman who enters this Illyrian world from the shipwreck I took to be about seventeen or eighteen years old, brought up with her twin brother Sebastian by their father (their mother is never mentioned in the play), a man, I felt, of great intelligence and warmth, since her relationship with her brother is so close and trusting. She has already learned (or inherited) that straightforward common sense, that unclouded attitude to life, that sense of being a person without prejudice – the qualities that are so wonderful about her. I suspect that the death of her father has been a great blow to her and that her relationship with her brother is all the stronger because of it. With him she is taking a summer cruise, we imagined, a tour in the royal yacht, and then the storm, and separation, and the rocky shore of Illyria, and the memory of her father's talk of Orsino and the decision to serve him as the sole link with the lost past.

Viola's disguise allows her to know Orsino in a way that would never have been possible otherwise. In three days he confides everything to this boy, this stranger, something he would never have done to a woman. The intimacy of confidence disturbs him – and this was something we tried hard to bring out in the production – the strange love for this boy is something that he cannot understand or explain. Viola is let into his mind, his confidence, his imagination, in such a way that inevitably she falls in love with him, with this extraordinary, erudite human being. The strange inevitability of Orsino's love for her was something we constantly tried to explore. Viola's greatest quality, her directness, is in one sense liberated, in another trapped, by her disguise, through which Viola not only reveals Orsino to himself, but also discovers herself. In three days she has 'unclasped the book' of his 'secret soul', has herself fallen desperately in love with him, and now allows the audience to follow her secret, and to be led through the play observing her journey and the increasing burden of her hidden love: 'Yet a barful strife! / Whoe'er I woo, myself would be his wife' (1.4.41–2). This sense of Viola entrapped by her disguise intensifies as the play goes forward, increasing the audience's eagerness for the resolution and Viola's own sense of helplessness. The character who has released others from self-obsession finds herself imprisoned. But it has been that ability to awaken others that has created the play. Without her nothing would go forward. Through her clarity, her simplicity, she releases from self-absorption, from death-obsession, Olivia and Orsino – by confronting them with themselves and what they are. Into the locked-up stillness of Illyria she brings life, and chaos, and hope; she is the catalyst of the play, stirring up the place, forcing them all up into a spiral, to wake up, to discuss, to learn about themselves, turning their world upside down. She arrives in Illyria like a life-force: 'What country, friends, is this?' (1.2.1).

The moment of Viola's entry changed significantly for me between Stratford and London. I tried to make the audience witness, as it were, to that terrible moment of loss, of parting from someone so close to her as her brother, by introducing a hopeless, helpless scream, almost of an animal, to bring focus immediately onto the pain of this person. In this short scene we see not only the initial pain, but also the positive qualities, her hope, her perception of others, her belief in the power of Time. In listening to the captain's story of Olivia, shutting the door, shunning life, I used to think that this could never happen to Viola, she would never do that, she does not think of men as a threat, emotionally or physically. Life for her is not to be lived behind locked doors. So from the idea of serving Olivia she turns to Orsino, to her memories of her father's talk of him, and then, instinctively, to the idea of disguise. She does not really know who she is – having lost her past she is in search of herself – she does not want to leave the place that provides the only hope of further news of her brother, and there in front of her is (or was in our production) Sebastian's trunk, which has been washed up with her. She opens it and finds his jacket, his doublet, and puts it on. And the smell of it, and the memory of him, means that in some way she keeps alive something of her brother, not just a piece of clothing but part of his soul, and by having that, through some sort of osmosis, the hope that he really is still alive is carried with her, always. 'Conceal me what I am', and her hope begins to flow back and she decides to wait, to trust to Time, to use the confidence and hope that is in her to change the situation. And so from the despair of its opening this little scene moves to its wonderfully optimistic conclusion: 'What else may hap, to time I will commit . . . Lead me on' (1.2.60, 64).

The meeting with Olivia, and the 'willow cabin' speech, were always difficult for me, rather like a horse going up to a jump, I used to feel. The scene is a conversation between two women, very different women, though similar in age, Olivia perhaps a little younger than Viola. It is just two women talking and you see the different perceptions of both of them, especially of Viola, who associates very strongly with Olivia's emotions (she too has lost a father and, she fears, a brother) and understands them. The apparent finality of Olivia's 'I cannot love him. / He might have took his answer long ago' (1.5.262–3) forces Viola into her big wooing speech; she has to make it, she has to do her appointed job, and she just happens to get carried away with it and so applies it to herself. And thus she admits to herself her love for Orsino by saying it out loud to another woman. The springboard for the willow cabin speech is her want, her need, to talk about her own love; it comes from the depth of her own imagination and she gets so carried away with it that she surprises herself. She has reached a new stage of self-awareness by the end of it.

On her way back from Olivia's house she is overtaken by Malvolio with the ring. She recognizes Olivia's motive, her self-delusion, immediately: 'She loves me sure' (2.2.22). What to do with this ring was the source of some discussion during our rehearsals, for it is never given back or referred to again. Eventually it was decided that I should hang it on a twig of the stage tree where it was found again by Feste at the end of the play. (Some members of the audience saw this as further evidence of Feste's secret love for Olivia, which they also thought they discerned at other points in the production.) As far as Viola is concerned, the significance of hanging the ring on the tree was primarily to be rid of something which she cannot accept without compromising herself. She cannot accept the responsibility of that ring, for the love which it implies is not truly given to her, should not be to her, and she does not want it to be to her. So she leaves it there for Time (or whoever) to discover, and with its rediscovery at the end we have the sense of the play coming full circle again. 'Time, thou must untangle this, not I' (2.2.40), she says as she takes stock of her situation, not a reckless surrender, but a declaration of trust and faith that Time, or something, is going to make things change. When we reach her next scene, however, her longest conversation with Orsino, she is losing that faith and touching her lowest point in the play.

The conversation between Orsino and Viola after the singing of 'Come away, death' I always felt a wonderfully close scene and an absolutely heartbreaking one. For here are two people in love who should love each other but cannot do so because one is incapable of seeing through disguises, not just hers but his own. Orsino deludes himself; he is blind about women and how they should be treated; supposes that they cannot be spoken to honestly or share the thoughts and feelings of men. Viola in this scene is, I think, in despair about her situation. All that Orsino says about women is so terrible for her to hear, so mistaken:

no woman's sides
Can bide the beating of so strong a passion
As love doth give my heart; no woman's heart
So big, to hold so much; they lack retention.   (2.4.93–6)

Her reply, I felt, was defensive, and angry – 'In faith, they are as true of heart as we' (2.4.106) – and the argument that follows catches her almost unawares. 'Ay, but I know' . . . 'What dost thou know?', and there she is nearly found out; through her unhappiness and frustration she has started into something and she has to explain: 'My father had a daughter lov'd a man' . . . to explain in the best way that she can . . . 'as it might be' . . . she's so close . . . 'as it might be, perhaps, were I a woman' . . . she is so close, so close to saying 'I am a woman, and I love you', but she has to disguise it, to disguise it in a way that tries to say to him that love is not about dying and despair, as he seems to perceive it. 'And what's her history?', he then asks, and that's when she realizes her situation: 'A blank, my lord; she never told her love.' That's something important, the difference between him and her; this is what might happen to her – never to speak, to remain silent and patient, for ever. 'But died thy sister of her love, my boy?' (line 119). He wants only to know about the misery of it all and she is trying to educate him, to take him in another direction that he has never perceived. But he cannot see, and she has to go around: 'I am all the daughters of my father's house, / And all the brothers too.' She is here, I think, near to despair. 'And yet I know not': the glimmer of hope is still there, but this always seemed to me her darkest moment. For Orsino, too, it is a strange moment, when he cannot decide, when he's nearly turned, and then habit, and confusion, and obsession take over again and he returns to his self-delusion: 'To her in haste . . . my love can give no place' (lines 123–4). At the end of the scene we see Viola, for almost the only time in the play, really depressed.

On the way to fulfil this gloomy mission, however, she meets Feste. The scene came after the interval in our production, at the top of the second act. Her relationship with Feste is another of the small joys of the play. He too is one of the play's outsiders: Malvolio, Feste, Antonio, Aguecheek, the Sea Captain, Viola – the play is full of loners. Feste, like all of Shakespeare's fools perhaps (but surely more so), has an extraordinary perception of life, an aptness of observation especially apparent in his scene with Orsino: 'changeable taffeta . . . thy mind is a very opal' (2.4.74–5) – he is exactly right about Orsino. And here, interrupted on her way to Olivia's, Viola contemplates the skill of the man who is 'wise enough to play the fool'

(3.1.60), and finds the diversionary pleasure of playing with words. She is always discovering things about life, and taking time off during the play to talk to the audience about them (now look at this person, isn't that interesting, isn't that wonderful, or odd), to share her sense of humour with them. Her relationship with Feste is an enjoyment of the mind – like her relationship with Orsino, if only they could break through to full understanding.

The chance of that comes by way of the recognition scene with Sebastian after her disguise has taken her through the comic absurdities of the mock duel with Aguecheek – comic and absurd for the audience, at least, though increasingly embarrassing and dangerous for Viola. The wonder of the recognition comes at an awful moment for her, as she is accused of having married Olivia, of beating Sir Andrew, wounding Sir Toby, denying the open-heartedness of Antonio's love, a crescendo of everything piling on top of her. And then, there is her brother like something out of a fairy story – just like a fairy story, indeed, that is what is so wonderful about it, the

13   Viola recognises Sebastian (Nigel Cooke)

sudden appearance of Sebastian, the apple cleft in twain, the mirror of herself. It is a magical moment, the resolution of confusion, the meeting of self, of each other; the whirlpool and the tempest that brought them to Illyria die down and suddenly there is wholeness again, the magical moment of seeing someone you thought was dead, the other half of yourself. 'Do not embrace me', she says (5.1.251), unable quite to make that contact whole until she knows again who she is by putting on her 'maiden's weeds', rediscovering that other half of herself through the ritual of dressing again as a woman.

After that comes Orsino's strangely hearty, and rather awkward, declaration:

> Boy, thou hast said to me a thousand times
> Thou never shouldst love woman like to me. (5.1.267–8)

Viola's reply is open and direct, honest and truthful as she has been throughout the play. In front of all those people she says:

> And all those sayings will I over swear,
> And all those swearings keep as true in soul
> As doth that orbed continent the fire
> That severs day from night. (5.1.269–72)

They are almost her last words in the play. I always thought it difficult for Orsino to make this sudden change from his obsession with Olivia, however carefully we had tried to prepare for it in the 'patience on a monument' dialogue. Viola (unlike Rosalind in *As You Like It*) is denied her 'woman's weeds'; there is no marriage ceremony, not even a formal offer from Orsino. 'Let me see thee in thy woman's weeds' he simply says, and a little later the bald statement that 'a solemn combination *shall* be made / Of our dear souls' (lines 383–4). The scene is a difficult one to make work, a director's nightmare (like the last scene of *Measure for Measure*, perhaps), and I do not think that our production ever really found it, though we worked hard at it and discussed and argued about it for two years! Perhaps the problem was just being a woman in 1983: putting out a hand to say I am going to marry you seemed an anti-climax. Whatever it was, our final scene never seemed to me thorough enough; it was never fully clear to the actors so could not be to the audience. It is a very public scene, everyone gathered together, a royal event with high and low characters all present and all their stories coming together, and I don't think we ever resolved its complexity or found the play's real ending. But then came the clap of thunder that marked the end of our production, and the returning darkness, and Feste finding the ring on the tree and singing of the wind and the rain. Things have come round full circle; they have reached a point of happiness – for some of the characters at least – but will they be happy ever after? It is the last verse of Feste's song that is so extraordinary.

I do not know how successful our production was; to be so involved in a play means that you can never fully know its effect on those watching. Like my first attempt at *Twelfth Night*, this one did not quite come up to hopes and expectations. Trying to write about it now I feel inadequate, and a little pompous. I am no authority; I can only try to do my best given the materials I have, the director, the set, the costume. *Twelfth Night* is a story about Time, and growing up, and growing old, beautiful, and elusive; and whichever way people try to direct it or to focus it so that it becomes a '1983 production', or so that you do it standing on your head, or hanging from the rafters, whatever you do as you dig and dig, and get deeper and deeper, the text remains for another attempt. I shall always be wanting to try it again.

Henry V

KENNETH BRANAGH

ENNETH BRANAGH played Henry V in Adrian Noble's production
in Stratford in 1984 and at the Barbican the following year. In the
same season, his first with the RSC, he was Laertes in *Hamlet* and
the King of Navarre in *Love's Labour's Lost*. In 1986 he directed and played
Romeo in *Romeo and Juliet* at the Lyric Theatre, Hammersmith. His
television work includes leading roles in Graham Reid's *Billy* trilogy, in *To
the Lighthouse*, and in *The Fortunes of War*; and his film performances
include a leading role in *A Month in the Country*. His own play *Public Enemy*
was produced at the Lyric Theatre, Hammersmith, in 1987. For the
Renaissance Theatre Company, of which he was a founder, he directed the
first of several Shakespeare productions, *Twelfth Night*, in 1987.

I was twenty-three years old when I came to play Henry V for the Royal
Shakespeare Company. The discussion of that experience which I now
embark upon is written at the grand old age of twenty-five. Therefore I feel
scarcely qualified to do more than give a very personal account of my own
particular approach to the part. Perhaps I should begin by setting that
approach in context and explain exactly where this young person came
from, and how he got the part in the first place. Both these factors had a
significant influence on the playing of the role.

My first experience of Henry V, inevitably, was Olivier's remarkable
film treatment. It would come to haunt me as I attempted the role myself,
but of that, more later. The first *real* encounter with the part and the play
was at drama school where I pitted my verse-speaking prowess (unsuccess-
fully!) against the rigours of 'Once more unto the breach', 'St Crispin's',
etc. Of course the classes at RADA allowed us to tackle a good many of the
purple passages from various plays in the canon, but nevertheless it was
here that a conviction grew about Henry, in particular. The obvious,
massive difficulties of some of the parts one tackled were clear. The
Macbeths and Antonys seemed palpably training exercises for a much later

'proper' attempt. But working on Henry's speeches I became convinced that although the technical and conceptual requirements were enormous, it was definitely a young man's part and *I* thought (given the right conditions) within my reach. However, a simple desire to play a particular part does not qualify a drama student for anything and soon my thoughts about the part were necessarily tucked away in face of the more immediate panic of finding a job. Any job.

I left RADA in December 1981. My Shakespearean experience was limited to the work on Henry V and others and finally augmented by a very swiftly spoken Hamlet which I gave in my final term. Professional good fortune was my happy lot on leaving drama school and for the next two years I worked steadily, first in the theatre and then on TV in a variety of roles. Indeed such was my luck that on two separate occasions when the Royal Shakespeare Company offered me work I was actually too busy to take it. Giddy with the success of regular employment I advised my agent on each occasion 'Say thank you very much and tell them I want to play Henry V.' There was a notable silence both times.

14   Kenneth Branagh as Henry with Exeter (Brian Blessed) and his staff, 1984

Finally in 1983 with a lucrative TV series just completed, I decided to use the money to create an opportunity for the classical acting challenge which my two Shakespeareless years of regular employment had robbed me of. It would test me in every way as an actor and if successful would be a useful vehicle with which to convince the RSC and all, that very young actors could do large verse parts! With two friends directing and designing, I learned and performed as a one man show, Tennyson's 1400 line monodrama *Maud* or *The Madness*. Thanks to Tennyson's neglected masterpiece and my two colleagues Kate Burnett and Colin Wakefield, the show was a great success and to my delight the Royal Shakespeare Company sent its spies. Soon a meeting was arranged to discuss the possibility of joining them to play, among other parts, Henry V.

When I met Barry Kyle and Adrian Noble, two of the company's directors, I was glad of having spent time on Henry at RADA. Keen though they were to have me in the company, Adrian had never seen me in a classical role and so asked if I would mind doing a speech of Henry's which I could go away and prepare. I said that I didn't mind and furthermore I would much rather do it there and then. They seemed delighted with the idea and so that November afternoon in 1983 on the stage of the Barbican Theatre I began my professional association with the hero of Agincourt. Staring out into a terrifyingly large and empty auditorium I began naturally enough with 'Once more unto the breach'. To the great surprise of Barry and Adrian I knew the speech off by heart, and so Adrian could experiment a little with directing me in it and assess whether the two of us could work together. I did it six different times with different notes from Adrian after each attempt.

Although at that stage it was inevitably a superficial experience the unadulterated thrill of working on such a part in a large theatre was a marvellous sensation and one which I revelled in throughout the following two years.

The meeting had gone well and aside from the pleasure of working with the two men, I was encouraged by their obvious eagerness to welcome a new generation of actors into the company in leading roles. It seemed that the 1984 season with Roger Rees as Hamlet, Antony Sher as Richard III, and Ian McDiarmid as Shylock would be an exciting one. I learnt the next day that the season would be opened by a production of *Henry V* in which a young and comparatively unknown actor called Kenneth Branagh would take the title role. Rehearsals would begin on 16 January 1984. In addition to Henry I would play the King of Navarre in *Love's Labour's Lost*, Laertes in *Hamlet* and take part in an as yet unwritten new play. I was thrilled and delighted and raring to go.

The month or so before rehearsals began seemed to me a very important time to take stock, as far as was possible, of exactly the progress (if any) I had made as an actor and how prepared I was to take on this challenge.

Significantly I was just coming to the end of an engagement at the Greenwich Theatre in London. I had been playing the title role in *Francis*, a new play by Julian Mitchell. It was a tough human account of the life of St Francis of Assisi. Although the company had worked together beautifully the unfashionable subject matter and a design which in retrospect seemed to work against the play combined to make the evening a critical failure. The experience was a salutary one for me on several counts. First it put into perspective my views about newspaper criticism of the theatre as it exists nowadays. So proud was I of the standard of the work and the attempt to do justice to the play that for the first time in my young career I did not feel myself compelled to buy the papers the next morning. The work itself had become far more important and far more satisfying. When I did learn, as one inevitably does through friends and fellow actors, that the notices had been vicious to all concerned, I felt completely able to take it on board and continue to work freely on something which I considered to be very fine. This may seem a slight point to make but for me it was a breakthrough and in the pressured times to come, opening a Stratford season, it was an invaluable source of strength to remember so graphically that 'the play's the thing'.

On *Francis* I also had the good fortune to work with a remarkably gifted director, David William. The clarity and perception of his views on acting gave my work a tremendous boost. I took many of his observations on with me into my preparation for Henry. He had known my work for some time and with our experience on *Francis* he was in a unique position to give the gentlest of progress reports. He made me aware of how I distributed acting energy. My preference and ease with the 'emotion of the here and now' and how, as on *Francis*, I must attend to the less easily captured qualities of 'remoteness' and spiritual isolation which such characters may experience and which Henry exhibits so clearly in 'Upon the King'. All this he made me believe was possible for a young actor if one continued to develop to the highest pitch one's imagination. The final breakthrough on *Francis* was the tentative beginnings of what I can only describe as a 'spiritual vocabulary': that openness and receptivity to the numinous which are so necessary to articulate and attempt to capture the humanity and size of spirit which

Francis of Assisi embodied. I looked forward to Henry determined to mine what I sensed also ran through every action of this similarly complex figure: huge reserves of compassion and, like Francis, a genuine visionary quality which I felt were necessary to make certain events in the play comprehensible.

The other mentor whose advice coloured my thinking on Henry was Hugh Cruttwell, the Principal of RADA during my time there. I remembered again his comments on preparing for Hamlet. The advice still held good. Assess the character as far as you are able. Hugh suggested using the Elizabethan 'humours' as a tool. Look at the character and the proportions of choler, phlegm, melancholia, sanguinity as they existed in him. Do the same for yourself and attend to the disparity. If nothing else it's a useful starting point on entering the mind of a man whose experiences are so very different from one's own. And finally I remembered Hugh's assessment of the three ingredients of great acting: passion, poetry, and humour. I knew the part of Henry V offered them all; it was my job to realise them.

The first rehearsal was conducted with only Adrian Noble and myself huddled either side of a gas heater in a cold hall near the Barbican. A small audience was made up of the Assistant Director A.J. Quinn and the Assistant Stage Manager Ian Barber. It was here that we talked through our first impressions of the play and the part. I read short passages aloud (registering inside how odd it felt to be actually *saying* these lines) and then we would use them as talking points. From the beginning we both agreed that the many paradoxes in the character should be explored as fully as possible. That we shouldn't try to explain them. I made clear my firm belief in the *genuine* nature of Henry's humility and piety. I also agreed that the man who threatens such violence before the gates of Harfleur was a professional killer of chilling ruthlessness.

> If not – why, in a moment look to see
> The blind and bloody soldier with foul hand
> Defile the locks of your shrill-shrieking daughters;
> Your fathers taken by the silver beards,
> And their most reverend heads dash'd to the walls;
> Your naked infants spitted upon pikes,
> Whiles the mad mothers with their howls confus'd
> Do break the clouds, as did the wives of Jewry
> At Herod's bloody-hunting slaughter-men.

> (3.3.33–41)

The terrifying warrior king that speaks so clearly through these lines threw another problem into focus. For so many people this play is dismissed as a crude glorification of militarism. I know many people who questioned the wisdom of putting the play on so soon after the Falklands conflict. And so on Day One we determined to throw aside the shackles of limiting pre-conceptions, remembering always to ask why those particular words are necessary to this king and how they exist in a man whose capacity for extraordinary compassion and forgiveness are self-evident in the rest of the play. Indeed all the early rehearsals had a genuine investigative, experimental quality to them. We had the luxury of a nine-week rehearsal period and Adrian was determined not to waste a second, nor to rush. Nothing in the play would be taken as understood, or overlaid by any 'modern' view. Everything would be questioned and our responses evaluated. It meant that we would do the play as honestly as we possibly could. It was a relief to me that we would not be burdened by the 'Post Falklands' tag that some of the press had already given the production. Our feelings about that conflict would inevitably inform our thoughts on the play but not to the point where the effect was reductive to the work.

The investigations were thorough and exhausting. In Henry's first scene Adrian's initial queries weren't about the text at all. He asked me why Henry hardly spoke in the scene and as he was to do throughout rehearsals he asked me about the scene Shakespeare didn't write. He was referring of course to the moment before the play begins when Henry is obviously told in private of the church's backing for an invasion of France. What was his reaction? And why in the first scene does he hold such a *public* discussion of what could already have been decided? I loved these challenges. For one, they threw one's attention (strangely enough) back on the text. And secondly they began to confirm for me an instinct I'd had about this young king's leadership, the importance of *how* things were done. *How* decisions were arrived at. The way in which his rule was *seen* to be carried out.

Perhaps simply the traits of a master politician? Yes, partly, but also the action of an intensely private man (I felt) forced to live completely outwardly – a life lived in public, under pressure from all sides in his own country because of his youth and past life and for whom the necessity of scrupulous honesty was an almost demonic drive within him. He had to prove himself doubly and 'Show them *how* to war', *if* war was necessary. How to war. How to war. I thought a great deal about Henry's view of that.

As we moved through the first week of rehearsal Adrian began to define more clearly how he saw the play in general terms. He referred to it as an Elizabethan Dream Play, written for a society to whom Henry V was a great English legend. He had been dead for nearly two centuries already and so the removes at which the story sits made certain aspects almost two-dimensional. He wanted to reflect this in the design he was working on with Bob Crowley. Their plan was to strip away the on-stage seating which had been a feature of Stratford settings for a few years and widen the forestage. It was here on what would be the widest (bar the Coliseum) forestage in the country, that he would stage the first section of the play. As the dream moved into France and for the English into nightmare he suggested the 'invasion' of the upstage area. The whole depth of the Stratford stage would be used to create a flexible black hole where the war would be fought. The design, however, was by no means fixed and I was glad that my own thoughts were taken into consideration at this early stage. I particularly liked the tapestry-like effect that the shallow and wide forestage area would give to the early part of the play. The notion of stripping the theatre down as much as possible to the bare boards and 'wooden O' seemed to me entirely in keeping with the spirit of the Chorus throughout. There was also a feeling that the differences between the two cultures in the play should be exploited visually with what little colour there would be, used mostly in costume. The sophisticated, elegant French finally emerged in rich blacks and golds in contrast to the roughly textured greys of the English. It was indicative of another healthy trait in the production's approach which was to tell the thrilling narrative of the piece as simply and clearly as possible without patronising the audience.

After a week or so of protected private work with Adrian, the rest of the company began to arrive. For me it was nerve-wracking but enjoyable. It took a certain pressure off me only to replace it with the equally frightening one of having to say the lines out loud in front of other actors! But not immediately. For a while we continued very informal discussions and exercises. I remember a particularly exciting version of the first scene with the archbishops and nobles performed as a modern day cabinet meeting. It was particularly useful in analysing Henry's political acumen. In a speech of such perfect balance he puts the cleric completely on the spot, forcing him and eventually the other members of the war cabinet, as it were, to reveal completely their attitudes to the prospective invasion:

> My learned lord, we pray you to proceed,
> And justly and religiously unfold
> Why the law Salique, that they have in France,
> Or should, or should not, bar us in our claim;
> And God forbid, my dear and faithful lord,
> That you should fashion, wrest, or bow your reading,
> Or nicely charge your understanding soul

With opening titles miscreate, whose right
Suits not in native colours with the truth. . .
Therefore take heed how you impawn our person,
How you awake our sleeping sword of war –
We charge you, in the name of God, take heed;
For never two such kingdoms did contend
Without much fall of blood, whose guiltless drops
Are every one a woe, a sore complaint,
'Gainst him whose wrongs gives edge unto the swords
That makes such waste in brief mortality.
Under this conjuration speak, my lord;
For we will hear, note, and believe in heart,
That what you speak is in your conscience wash'd
As pure as sin with baptism.   (1.2.9–32)

He flatters the Archbishop at the same time reminding this most unholy of holy men of the price of perjury. In the middle section there is an almost soliloquised quality, a moral *gravitas* which suggested to me genuine emotional weight given to the thought of the deaths involved in what is being discussed. For Henry it *is* completely real. Having been fighting since the age of twelve in a world where combat was hand to hand – bloody and savage – knowledge of the reality of war must be seen to be with him from the very beginning. The concern is great and suffused with his own terrible experience. He sees further than the Archbishop will ever do, and yet he chooses to meet the Archbishop on his own terms and contain his vision and wisdom in language of polite precision. And as always the speech is permeated by the humility of a man for whom always must go 'God before'. He is a *genuinely* holy man and it seemed to me ridiculous to play him as some one-dimensional Machiavell. I was reminded once again that if we could convince the audience of the man's *practical* faith whilst admitting his political brilliance they would be forced to think anew about the play just as we had chosen to rehearse it afresh. I resolved once again that as complex a figure as this, engendering as he does so many ambivalent feelings, would not be given a performance which tried to explain him. The audience for the show would have to do that for themselves. I continued to remind myself of this, writing regularly in the margin 'Do not judge this man, place him in context – *understand!*'

Understanding was not the easiest thing to achieve in the early weeks of rehearsal as my mind was awhirl with confused thoughts about the character and the play and increasingly about the technical demands of the text. Each time I stumbled over a word in rehearsal there was a cry of terror inside as I imagined making similar gaffes in front of 1500 people at

Stratford. Early on I consulted the two RSC voice coaches, David Carey and Cis Berry. Both made themselves available to me regularly and I am eternally grateful for the technical assistance they gave. Both reminded me from their particular standpoint of the inextricable bond between textual understanding and technical accuracy. More often than not, if I was continually running out of breath at the end of a particular line, it was more to do with not having the character's thought and intention clear than insufficient intake of breath. If I could find out *why* I was saying something then they could help me with *how* I should serve it vocally. A reminder of these ABCs was a great confidence-giver. It was through these sessions also that one could explore, in releasing physical exercises and experiments, the emotional weight of the words in the play which recurred over and over again and which were obsessing me: peace, death, war, God, and especially honour. A correct and full definition of this idea in terms of Henry V was fundamental to my interpretation. His own personal concept of honour seemed fuelled by tremendous repression. He was unable to release huge amounts of humour and indeed of violence. The responsibility of kingship which he takes so profoundly seriously keeps all such human expressions contained, but all the more charged and dangerous. When such qualities are released we see them at their extremes. An example of these qualities and their juxtaposition comes in the middle of the play. With 'Once more unto the breach' Henry is a soldier working brilliantly on his feet in the middle of battle. This passionate speech of persuasion contains all the noble thoughts, allied to action, that make a glorious leader. The images pour into one another, vibrant and exciting; the appeal to the senses is irresistibly put.

Compare this zenith of the fighting man with the desperate nadir that follows it in the speech to the Governor of Harfleur. Here Henry is a desperate man in the midst of a siege gone terribly wrong. The lines are threatening, unforgiving, and indicative I believe of an awesome personal capacity for violence. Similarly, in the speech to Scroop and the traitors we see another extreme of emotion unleashed. This time the act of personal treachery produces a tremendous sense of hurt, expressed at great length and fuelled by genuine emotion and once again the need to make example of any betrayal of the *way* in which Henry would war. With each of these dramatic moments in the interior journey of the man through the play I sought to reveal his vision. A man who saw far beyond individual acts, assessing their often terrible consequences, and *feeling* them as a man, as a political leader, and as a Christian king.

As the weeks passed it was no easier to put such instinctive feelings into practice. Often my fledgling attempts to encompass the scale of such a work would turn into rants during the violent bits and inaudible mumbling in the gentler passages. Throughout, my director and the rest of the cast were patient and encouraging. They were qualities maintained throughout the run which allowed me the wonderful luxury of experimenting, and hopefully improving the gap between what I saw so clearly possible in the part and what at that stage I was able to achieve. Indeed the truly organic nature of Adrian's rehearsals engendered a mutually supportive company feeling which paid wonderful dividends in our long relationship with the play. Throughout the run from start to finish there were endless healthy discussions and new insights into the characters and the various scenes, a marvellous creative atmosphere. It lessened my own personal paranoia about having to 'prove myself' as an actor and therefore helped my playing of the role immeasurably over the long months of the Stratford season.

I had been keeping a rehearsal log during the early weeks, a taped diary into which I would pour my thoughts at the end of each rehearsal day. After five weeks I found myself so completely exhausted in the evenings that I was barely able to talk, let alone speak coherently about an increasingly complex rehearsal period on the most difficult role I'd ever encountered. My recollection therefore of the weeks that led up to the opening night is hazy. There were unforgettable moments, however. The joyous camaraderie of the company led to wonderful moments of revelation, as when we discovered *en masse* the power of having Bardolph executed on stage in front of the king. The first time we played it in rehearsal was thrilling. For me it shed a whole new light on Henry's loneliness, marking so graphically, as it did, the end of a chapter of events which robbed him of every real friend he had, Falstaff, Scroop, and now symbolically all who remained to remind him of the Boar's Head life. He was now completely alone with a solitude so painful that it must produce 'Upon the King' and which can only be partly alleviated by the meeting with Katherine – one of the few people in the play, paradoxically, who is in a position to understand Henry. It characterised also yet another test of Henry's character: it would have been easy for Henry quietly to have pardoned the man for stealing from a church. But aside from how personally Henry would have felt this affront to God, once again there was the question of example. As in the traitors' scene, the army would have known of the king's relationship with the man and he was therefore under intense scrutiny. To have pardoned a former friend would have spelt disaster for the discipline of the beleaguered army. Bardolph must die but not, I felt, without intense personal cost to the king and this is what we chose to dramatise. It seemed to me unsentimental, but an extremely painful moment in the lives of all involved in that complex story. I hoped in doing so we were meeting the challenge of the play and illuminating the dramatic events and contradictory emotions of the war. And so as the king I took in the awful sight and found from somewhere the reserves of emotion to carry on, leaving the *man* Henry deeply shaken and the *king* Henry resolved.

There were other exciting moments. A Hitchcockian traitors' scene drew out every ounce of the demonic showman that also lies in Henry. And there was the constant turmoil of thought on how to approach 'Upon the King', and indeed all of the night-time section of the play. I think I finally came to the conclusion that Henry answers no question in that scene and the 'Upon the King' soliloquy emerges because of the terrible certainty of what Williams has said. There will never be any real contact between him and other men however he may persuade them of the rightness of particular acts. They will never have any real desire or inclination to understand him or what he does. It's the confirmation that he will be forever utterly alone.

15   Henry and Katherine (Cécile Paoli) in Act 5, Scene 2

Only God and the eventual enlightenment (no more) that 'Upon the King' brings him will give any sort of comfort.

As I look back on the experience I am continually reminded of how amazingly rich I found the character. Apart from these wonderful purple patches there was the joy of establishing the clarity of Henry's relationships with others – with Exeter in the heart-warming form of Brian Blessed and, most interestingly, with the Mountjoy of Christopher Ravenscroft. He provided beautifully a barometer of the French reaction to this upstart king and gave human substance to the relationship between king and diplomat. Finally, of course, in *Henry V* there is the wooing scene which was an especial joy to rehearse and play with Cécile Paoli and Yvonne Coulette. It was almost the greatest challenge in the performance to make credible that this was the same man whom we had seen throughout the play. In the end Shakespeare provided as usual the simplest answer, and we played the scene to the hilt on the simplest of premises, that the two characters do not speak each other's language but do literally in the course of one brief interview fall in love. This despite Henry having disposed of most of the French Royal Family.

Of the events concerning the opening of the production I can remember little that is useful here. I did not read the notices immediately. I learnt enough, however, to give myself the dubious pleasure of looking at most of them a little later in the season. As I played through the 139 performances that the production gave, my own performance changed a great deal. I became, naturally enough I suppose, much stiller physically and therefore probably more kingly. I grew in confidence technically and felt much more able to 'play the house'. Indeed after about 60 performances so dramatic did I consider the improvement in my own work over the period that I shuddered to think what I had been like early on! The strengthening of the off-stage relationships informed the on-stage work and I watched with pleasure the other strands of this epic (from which structurally my character was quite divorced) with great pleasure, the Chorus, the low life scenes, the French. As time went on I also felt the piece more painful to play, the feeling of desolation in the play more palpable. It was humbling to confirm the hope that what seemed much more than a historical pageant turned out to be a profoundly moving debate about war.

That, however, is only my view and, as some may regard my view of the character, perhaps an idealistic one. Certainly this account of the experience of playing it reveals, I suppose, a very instinctive and emotional approach. It was, I must confess, an oddly emotional experience to look at the text again in preparing for this essay. It pitched me back immediately into that world where vital emotions were so near the surface and lived through at a time when my own were very thrown by the onset of responsibility and a kind of fame, where the compassion of the piece and its unrelenting toughness offered solace of a kind for an often bewildered young actor. It was a remarkable experience.

Mercutio in
Romeo and Juliet

ROGER ALLAM

ROGER ALLAM played Mercutio in John Caird's production of *Romeo and Juliet* on the RSC's regional tour in 1983 and at The Other Place at Stratford in 1984. On the same tour he was Theseus and Oberon in *A Midsummer Night's Dream*. He first joined the RSC in 1981 when his work included parts in *All's Well that Ends Well* and *Titus Andronicus*. Earlier Shakespearean roles had been Angelo in *Measure for Measure* and Macbeth. For the RSC in 1984–5 his roles included Clarence in *Richard III* and in 1985–6 Javert in *Les Misérables*, at the Barbican and later in the West End. At Stratford in 1987 he played Brutus, Sir Toby Belch, and the Duke in *Measure for Measure*.

I was offered the part of Mercutio early in 1983, and there were many reasons why it was an important turning point for me. It was the first good Shakespearean part I played with the Royal Shakespeare Company, and was a role which from the start I felt an affinity towards. *Romeo and Juliet* was to be one half of the 1983 regional tour, an area of the RSC's work to which I was, and am, particularly committed. Sheila Hancock, the tour's artistic director, involved myself and some other actors in the Barbican company, by discussing with us, as a group, the general idea of the tour, the choice of plays, the need for a vigorous barnstorming style and attitude given that we were playing in a motley collection of town halls, leisure centres, gymnasiums, and the like. So I was in at the planning stage, an unusual position for an actor at the RSC. Later on, Sheila asked me to play the double of Oberon and Theseus in *A Midsummer Night's Dream*. It became an offer I could not refuse. There were, however, many months between offer and rehearsal. I was meant to be working right up to when we started in August, but because Trevor Nunn's production of *All's Well that Ends Well*, in which I played a small character role, closed early on Broadway, I not only had this long period to get to know both plays, but also two months of leisure in which there was nothing else to occupy my

16   Roger Allam as Mercutio with Romeo (Simon Templeman), 1984

energies. I began to recall my own experience when I was Mercutio's age (late teens I decided, a year or two older than Romeo) as a pupil at a public school called Christ's Hospital. This school is situated in the idyllic countryside of the Sussex Weald, just outside Horsham. I recalled the strange blend of raucousness and intellect amongst the cloisters, the fighting, the sport, and general sense of rebelliousness, of not wishing to seem conventional (this was the sixties); in the sixth form (we were called Grecians) the rarefied atmosphere, the assumption that of course we would go to Oxford or Cambridge; the adoption of an ascetic style, of Zen Buddhism, of baroque opera, the Velvet Underground, Frank Zappa, and Mahler; of Pound, Eliot and e. e. cummings. We perceived the world completely through art and culture. We were very young, very wise, and possessed of a kind of innocent cynicism. We wore yellow stockings, knee breeches, and an ankle length dark blue coat, with silver buttons. We had read Proust, we had read Evelyn Waugh, we knew what was what. There was a sense, fostered by us and by many teachers, that we were already up there with Lamb, Coleridge, and all the other great men who had been educated there. We certainly thought that we soared 'above a common bound'. I suppose it is a process of constant mythologising that is attempted at any public school. *Tom Brown's Schooldays* is a good example. Girls were objects of both romantic and purely sexual, fantasy; beautiful, distant, mysterious, unobtainable, and, quite simply, not there. The real vessel for emotional exchange, whether sexually expressed or not, were our own intense friendships with each other. The process of my perceptions of Mercutio intermingling with my emotional memory continued intermittently, up to and including rehearsals. I am now aware that possibly I reconstructed my memory somewhat, mythologised it even, excising what was irrelevant, emphasising what was useful, to accord with how I was beginning to see the part, and what I wanted to express with it. What I was seeing in Mercutio was his grief and pain at impending separation from Romeo, so I suppose I sensitised myself to that period of my life when male bonding was at its strongest for me.

All's Well finished its run by the end of May, and so, funded by inflated Broadway wages, I did not need to work and took a holiday in Italy. I spent a week in Venice, staggered by the confidence and wealth of its past, drinking in its painting and architecture. As I looked at the paintings in the Accademia from Byzantine to Mannerist, I felt I was witnessing the emergence of an ever more complex view of the world, alongside the means to express that complexity in oil paint, and through the use of angle, colour and light. I felt a vivid sense of the correspondence between this visual richness and the developing language of English drama and poetry in the sixteenth and seventeenth centuries. Making visual connections is very important to many actors as we have become used to appreciating complexity of meaning expressed as a stream of pictures in film. Personally I play and re-play sections of my favourite films on a video machine, analysing obsessively the detailed visual choices of actors and directors. For me, standing in front of a Botticelli or a Veronese was like seeing a Shakespeare speech brought to life, a kind of visual equivalent which stimulated my feeling for the world of the play. I went south to a rented farmhouse in the Chianti hills near Siena. Italy still has a provincial sophistication that comes from its long history as a collection of city states. That, combined with a hot climate, means that the Italians occupy their streets and squares with much greater ease than the English. The resultant street life is very rich, even in small towns like Arrezo and Giaole, fertile ground for the peeping Tom aspect of an actor's preparation. I took many trips to Siena, and was struck by its beauty, but also by the beauty of the Siennese themselves. They are dark, fierce, and aristocratic, very different to the much paler Venetians or Florentines. They have always looked like this, as the paintings of their ancestors testify. I observed the groups of young people, the lounging grace with which they wore their clothes, their sense of always being on show. I walked the streets, they paraded them. It did not matter that I do not speak a word of Italian; I made up stories about them, and took surreptitious photographs. I was in Siena on the final day of the Palio, a lengthy festival ending in a horse race around the main square. Each district is represented by a horse and jockey and a pair of flag-bearers. The day is spent by teams of supporters with drums, banners, and ceremonial horse and rider processing round the town singing a strange chanting song. Outside the Cathedral, watched from a high window by a smiling Cardinal and a group of nuns, with a huge crowd in the Cathedral Square itself, the supporters passed, and to drum rolls the two flag-bearers hurled their flags high into the air and caught them, the crowd roaring its approval. The winner of the extremely dangerous horse race is presented with the palio, a standard bearing the effigy of the Virgin. In the last few years the jockeys have had to be professional by law, as when they were amateurs, corruption and bribery were rife. The teams wear a curious fancy dress, encompassing styles from the twelfth to the eighteenth centuries. They are followed by gangs of young men, supporters, who create an atmosphere of intense rivalry and barely suppressed violence as they run through the narrow streets in the heat of the day. It was perfect. I took many more photographs. At the farmhouse that evening, after far too much Chianti, I and my friends played a bizarre game. In the dark, some of us moved lighted candles from one room to another, whilst others watched the effect of the light on faces and on the rooms from outside. It was like a strange living film of the paintings we had seen. Maybe Derek Jarman was spying on us.

I write about this at some length, because my experience at that time became inextricably linked with what I brought to Mercutio. I am aware that I was coming up with a version of Italy to suit my needs, much as I was doing with my memory. Any tourist does that. Looking back, perhaps I came into rehearsals with too much data swilling about my brain, like an overcrowded soup. Perhaps it prevented me from sharing and discovering as openly as possible with John Caird, the director, and, more importantly, my fellow actors. I know I have never had so much leisure between being offered a part, and starting rehearsals. Certainly to get to know the play, whilst recalling my own adolescence, in the atmosphere of Tuscany, is a heady mix. It was this smaller part, rather than the larger challenge of Oberon/Theseus, that I became obsessive about before rehearsals. I was fortunate to be sharing this time with my dearest friend Susan Todd, a theatre director, so that all my perceptions about the past, Italy, and the play I could examine and test with her.

In reading the play I noticed how, through its different characters and their attitudes, it seemed to ask what the true value of love is, and whose valuation of it we are inclined to accept. Shakespeare often uses a key word to express an idea. In *The Merchant of Venice* it is 'bond', in *Romeo and Juliet* it is 'bound'. Romeo speaks of love as being 'bound, shut up in a prison', Capulet says 'Montague is bound as well as I', Lady Capulet speaks of 'unbound lover', in the sense of being incomplete like an unbound book. Mercutio wants Romeo to 'soar . . . above a common bound', a phrase that reminded me very much of my own youthful pretensions. Once Romeo is beloved by Juliet he is unbound and can 'o'erperch these walls' with 'love's light wings'. Because Juliet's 'bounty is as boundless as the sea', she does not want Romeo to 'swear', to be bound lightly, in that context, although she does seek marriage, to be truly bound. I made connections with other Shakespeare plays, *The Merchant of Venice*, *As You Like It*, *Love's Labour's Lost*, which centralise the action of the female educating the male to the true and serious nature of loving relationships between the sexes, only of course in this story with tragic results. Mercutio seems obsessed with destroying Romeo's romantic view of love, and always speaks of love for women crudely and reductively in terms of sex. His repetitive use of sexual punning seemed neurotic to me, and I saw it as springing from his sense of loss, that Romeo was irrevocably changing, that their own friendship could not 'soar above a common bound', that his closest, most passionate, and intense relationship was ending. A similar, but more explored, version of this psychic battle goes on in *The Merchant of Venice*, between Antonio, Bassanio, and Portia. I noticed the young men's use of language; that even when Mercutio is at his crudest in sexual terms, there is a brilliant and inventive linguistic wit on the surface. Romeo's language has a similar punning quality, which deepens and becomes more emotionally direct as he is loved by Juliet.

As rehearsals began, I was fortunate in establishing an easy rapport with Daniel Day-Lewis and James Simmons (Romeo and Benvolio respectively), not dissimilar on the surface to our characters' relationships in the play. I discovered later that all three of us went to public schools. Ilona Sekazc's music played an important part in our production, and as a number of us played musical instruments, this was incorporated into the production as well. So, at the beginning of Act I, Scene 4, we entered grotesquely masked, myself playing the guitar, Jimmy Yuill's Balthazar dressed up as a blind Cupid, singing a raucous Latin song. This was to be our masquerade for the ball. The basic physical objective of the scene is to go in to the dance, an objective on which Romeo is consistently pouring cold water. Mercutio's and Benvolio's differing attitudes to Romeo's melancholy are very quickly established in the scene; Benvolio is placatory, Mercutio irritated and sardonic. Up to the beginning of the Queen Mab speech a rapid verbal sparring takes place in which Mercutio quickly establishes his reductive attitude to Romeo's love for Rosaline: 'Prick love for pricking, and you beat love down.' He also refers to love as a 'mire . . . wherein thou stickest up to the ears' (1.4.28, 41). The tempo quickens until Romeo claims that it is not good sense to go to the masque as he has had a dream. This starts the argument and arc of the Queen Mab speech. I had never seen *Romeo and Juliet* on the stage before, and had only seen the Zeffirelli film as a schoolboy. I was, however, aware that Mercutio was traditionally seen as being somehow taken over by his own extraordinary invention in this speech. This never seemed the case to me. Romeo and Mercutio are having an argument about feeling versus intellect. Mercutio is disgusted and betrayed that Romeo is putting his faith in love and dreams: 'dreamers often lie'. This argument between them continues right to the end of the scene. The first section of the speech builds up a brilliant and witty picture of Queen Mab. John Caird suggested that it was like some insane Jackanory nursery tale, and indeed this was how we did it, myself seated on a bench, the others on the floor around me: Mercutio doing one of his turns. The tension drops, everyone relaxes. It seems irrelevant to the preceding argument as the picture gets more and more detailed, almost pedantically so, as Mab's waggon spokes, covers, traces, collars, whip, and waggoner are itemised. Mercutio now commands the attention of the group:

> And in this state she gallops night by night
> Through lovers' brains, and then they dream of love.   (1.4.70–1)

This I took to be the central moment, and I put a substantial pause in the middle of the second line while staring accusingly at Romeo. The images get sharper and more satirical as the picture now builds up of Mab being that tiny germ which makes everyone behave according to their mould – conventionally, materialistically, boringly; that which makes courtiers obsequious, lawyers grasping, ladies flirtatious and prey to the gratification of their appetite for sweet things; a soldier a braggart and a coward; a parson think only of his tithes.

The images get darker and more sexually nightmarish as Mercutio goads Romeo and tries to get some response:

> This is the hag, when maids lie on their backs,
> That presses them and learns them first to bear,
> Making them women of good carriage.   (1.4.92–4)

Having started with a lover dreaming of love, the speech ends in a misogynistic image of rape and pregnancy, which at last gets a response from Romeo:

> ROMEO   . . . Thou talk'st of nothing.
> MERCUTIO   True, I talk of *dreams*,
>   Which are the children of an *idle brain*,
>   Begot of *nothing* but *vain fantasy*,
>   Which is as thin of substance as the air,
>   And more *inconstant* than the wind.   (1.4.96–100)

By placing his faith in 'dreams', feeling, love for women, Romeo is being 'inconstant' to Mercutio. He is betraying a relationship based on a higher, truer love, the bond between men. I did most of the second half of the speech directed very strongly at Romeo. When he, finally responding, got up and moved away, I leapt to my feet following him, shouting 'True I talk of dreams', very hurt and angry. After Benvolio's ineffectual attempt to be placatory, Romeo takes up the argument and rejects Mercutio. His dream is a dark premonition of early death. John Caird made the useful comment that this speech was equivalent to Romeo saying 'There are more things in heaven and earth, Mercutio, than are dreamt of in your philosophy.' 'But he that hath the steerage of my course / Direct my sail.' Romeo is fatalistic and filled with foreboding, but will not change his course of action. Mercutio wants to take control of his own destiny with his intellect and not be 'Mab-led'. Queen Mab links in this way with the central theme of fate in the play. She is also, perhaps, that irrationality that fuels and keeps alive the 'ancient grudge'. The scene is difficult as one is thrust right into the middle of Mercutio's and Romeo's relationship, but once I had perceived Mercutio as being hurt and indeed jealous of Romeo's love for Rosaline, I did not then find the Queen Mab speech isolated, but part of a continuing and passionate argument, and therefore possible to make sense of.

Although we have nothing to say in the next scene, Act 1, Scene 5, Mercutio and Benvolio were very much leaders of the revels. I played the guitar, Benvolio a drum, both dancing and singing more Latin songs, wearing the masks of the previous scene. This was useful preparation for Act 2, Scene 1, as I could actually experience, to some degree, the exhilaration and excitement of that expenditure of energy at a party, after which one is left drunk out in the street at about three in the morning. This seemed right for my physical and mental state in the next scene. Mercutio brings back on stage the feelings of hurt between himself and Romeo, that are unresolved at the end of Act 1, Scene 4. The information that Romeo has 'leapt this orchard wall' (2.1.5), presumably in pursuit of Rosaline, sparks off the bitterness again. Once more Mercutio's emotional pain is filtered and expressed through a series of rapid, cruel, witty, misogynistic jokes. It is an attempt to call Romeo back both actually and metaphorically from danger. The conventional image of the lover is again mocked. I sang some of these lines to an impromptu guitar accompaniment. As is often the case, a number of elements came together to produce this piece of stage business. The scene is a string of extremely explicit sexual jokes. Brian Gibbons, the editor of the invaluable Arden edition, uses the somewhat understated phrase 'with a bawdy quibble' to indicate this. It made us laugh very much in rehearsals. We invented a pastiche Elizabethan song called 'with a bawdy quibble', which was sung in cod operatic tones to the guitar. It made us laugh even more. As I was playing the guitar in the production anyway, it was a short step to introduce the idea into the scene itself. It became an extension of Mercutio's purely verbal virtuosity. And anyway it got a huge laugh to say 'He heareth not', after that assault on the eardrums. Much use is made in the scene of the word 'conjure': 'conjure' in the sense of invocation, trying to make Romeo actually appear, and also punning on the sense of conjuring up and conjuring down an erection. It is a short step, in punning terms, from conjure to conjugal. Mercutio first conjures Romeo to appear by itemising Rosaline, and reducing her to her physical parts: forehead, lips, foot, leg, thigh, vagina.

> . . . 'twould anger him
> To raise a spirit in his mistress' circle,
> Of some strange nature, letting it there stand
> Till she had laid it and conjur'd it down.
> That were some spite. (2.1.23–7)

By violating the object of Romeo's love, Mercutio can revenge himself on Romeo for leaving him, all in bitter jest, of course.

> . . . My invocation
> Is fair and honest; in his mistress' name
> I conjure only but to raise up him. (lines 27–9)

He is ironically aware that the only way he can give Romeo an erection is by naming the physical attributes of Rosaline. Mercutio's drunkenness and sense of loss reveal confusion around the sexuality of his relationship to Romeo, a sexuality that neither he nor Romeo allow:

> O, Romeo, that she were, O that she were
> An open-arse and thou a pop'rin pear! (lines 37–8)

Here Mercutio almost pleads. If only Romeo's love for women were purely sexual, 'an open-arse' and 'a pop'rin pear', then Mercutio would not feel so threatened. Women as sex objects he can cope with, as rivals for Romeo's love he cannot.

Romeo's line 'He jests at scars that never felt a wound' not only ironically prefigures the nature of Mercutio's death, but also suggests that Romeo is unaware of the depth of Mercutio's feelings for him. Throughout the scene, Benvolio continues his placatory function, his love for Romeo being of a far simpler kind, and requiring less affirmation than Mercutio's. This scene is very dense and packed with meaning. The discovery of Mercutio's physical state was a great help in unlocking it for me. He is drunk, it is after a party, late at night, all of which heighten his emotional hurt and confusion. The double irony is that Mercutio does not know that Juliet is now the object of Romeo's love.

Act 2, Scene 4, is the following morning. Mercutio is very quickly informed by Benvolio that Romeo has not been home all night and that, by letter, Tybalt has challenged Romeo to a duel. For Mercutio these two facts are immediately connected. Romeo obviously 'leapt this orchard wall' to try and see Rosaline. Tybalt has somehow found out. 'Alas, poor Romeo, he is already dead, stabb'd with a white wench's black eye, run through the ear with a love-song, the very pin of his heart cleft with the blind bow-boy's butt-shaft' (2.4.13–16). Mercutio equates Romeo's love for Rosaline with death through fighting Tybalt. Tybalt is, however, a more tangible enemy: 'and is he a man to encounter Tybalt?' The thought begins to form in Mercutio's mind that he could fight Tybalt in Romeo's stead. Fight him, beat him, and, as it were, psychically win back Romeo by saving him physically. He can literally fight for Romeo's life. Although Mercutio can mock Tybalt for being the over-correct 'fashion monger', he is also 'More than Prince of Cats . . . a duellist, a duellist', a very real danger. Interestingly it is the youthful Tybalt who, more than any other character in the play, is most active in keeping alive the 'ancient grudge'. Romeo enters (2.4.35). After the by-now-usual mocking diatribe on conventional love, 'Laura to his lady was a kitchen wench', Mercutio tries to discover through much sexual innuendo precisely what did happen the previous night. Romeo, however, responds in kind: 'O single-sol'd jest, solely singular for the singleness'. Gone is the morose adolescent, 'bound' by love; here is the old Romeo, witty and affectionate. The joking takes over: 'Why, is this not better now than groaning for love? Now art thou sociable'. A joyous speech, the bitterness and hurt of the previous night are gone: 'now art thou Romeo; now art thou what thou art' . . . I held his face between my hands . . . 'by art as well as by nature'. I joked to undercut and conceal my own sincerity: 'for this drivelling love is like a great natural that runs lolling up and down to hide his bauble in a hole'. Mercutio again equates love for women with mechanical mindless sex. 'I was come to the whole depth of my tale, and meant indeed to occupy the argument no longer.' Mercutio wins first prize for inserting more 'bawdy quibbles' in one sentence than any other Shakespeare character. The entrance of the Capulets' Nurse and her request for 'some confidence' with Romeo sparks off further bawdy quibbling at her expense: 'A bawd, a bawd, a bawd! So ho!' Sub-textually for Mercutio, her link with Romeo must confirm that Romeo has indeed become Rosaline's secret lover and that the Nurse is the go-between (not too far from the truth). Tybalt has found out, so there is the reason for the duel. Romeo now seems his old self, his love for Rosaline does not now seem so threatening to Mercutio, perhaps it has become purely sexual, the 'open-arse' and the 'pop'rin pear', the 'bauble in a hole'. Tybalt remains a very real danger; if Mercutio can remove him, he will bind Romeo to himself still further. I did this rather pedantic reasoning, as it was important for me as an actor to string together consistent psychological reasons for Mercutio to intervene in the duel, which is quite clearly what he intends at the start of Act 3, Scene 1.

Benvolio is unaware of Mercutio's intentions, and, again placatory, tries to get him home and out of trouble. As Benvolio is obviously not the quarrelsome character that Mercutio describes, I used the next few speeches as a ploy to keep him and our companions from leaving. Mercutio is buying time until Tybalt arrives. His verbal invention creates both a ludicrously unlikely picture of Benvolio and also comments ironically on

17   Mercutio and the Nurse (Polly James)

himself: 'What eye but such an eye would spy out such a quarrel?' (3.1.21).
On Tybalt's entrance Mercutio immediately tries to pick a fight: 'Couple it
with something, make it a word and a blow' and 'Here's my fiddlestick,
here's that shall make you dance' (lines 39, 48). But Tybalt is resistant, and
then Romeo enters. John Caird rightly made Romeo's refusal to fight as
difficult as possible. Tybalt brutally slapped him and finally spat in his
face. This gives Mercutio a clear opportunity to intervene, but crucially
alters his motive. For myself, Mercutio does not want Romeo to fight
Tybalt, as Tybalt is a very dangerous duellist. He does, however, want
Romeo to want to fight Tybalt. The fact that he doesn't proves to Mercutio
that Romeo is still 'bound' by love. If Rosaline were purely a sexual object
then Romeo would not say to Tybalt 'good Capulet – which name I tender /
As dearly as mine own'. In Mercutio's terms, Romeo has been unmanned
by love. It is impossible to play all the myriad reasons why Mercutio still
takes up the gauntlet, but they form the foundation for the final impulse to
draw a sword, and risk death. In the end the physical situation gives you
that: it is very hot, you are faced by an enemy you despise, who has just
humiliated your dearest friend. The fight is a scene in itself, and we were
lucky to have Malcolm Ransom as fight director, who always conceives his
fights in terms of character. 'Tybalt is "a duellist, a duellist"', Mercutio a
fighter' said Malcolm. This simple observation enabled us to characterise
very clearly the streetwise Mercutio and the punctilious Tybalt. At one
point, for instance, Mercutio hit Tybalt in the groin, disarming him and
thereby making the watchers think he had won. It enabled us to take
Mercutio's wit into his fighting, by constantly mocking Tybalt's correct-
ness and playing to the gallery. But for Romeo's intervention Mercutio
could have won. Malcolm was very helpful in solving Mercutio's death as
well. Is Mercutio aware that he is dying, but still joking? Are Romeo and
Benvolio aware? Malcolm confronted this problem when he was doing the
play at the Sheffield Crucible. A stagehand showed him a T-shirt with one
small red blot on the front and on the back. He had been a builder working
on a site using a nailgun. A nail had ricocheted from the concrete right
through his body, passing through his lung. He felt a sharp pain then
carried on with his work. A minute later he was choking as his lung filled
with blood. Luckily he was rushed to hospital just in time. This was perfect
for Mercutio. Tybalt's rapier pierces his lung on 'I am hurt' (line 90). He
still thinks it's serious on 'Go, villain, fetch a surgeon.' The initial pain
passes; he looks at the wound, there is the merest spot of blood. 'No'
(pause) ''tis not so deep as a well, nor so wide as a church-door.' He does a

turn, the mock-heroic duellist, with sly asides to Romeo: 'I am pepper'd, I warrant, for this world', 'a plague a' both your houses'. He shouts after Tybalt: 'a villain, that fights by the book of arithmetic'. Suddenly he chokes, and coughs up blood onto his handkerchief. 'Why the devil came you between us? I was hurt under your arm' (lines 102–3). Agonisingly he realises that Romeo has caused his death. 'Your houses!', his final cry, still refers to the pointless, 'Mab-led', 'ancient grudge' which has caused his death. The huge irony for Mercutio is that he never knows about Juliet, although he is acutely aware of the effect that true love has had on Romeo. The huge irony for Romeo is that Mercutio does succeed in piling up an emotional debt which forces Romeo to avenge Mercutio's death by killing Tybalt. By his death Mercutio does, then, force himself between Romeo and Rosaline/Juliet, and start a chain reaction that destroys them both. The infuriated and destructive impulse that leads Mercutio to his death shows that he too is prey to the 'Mab-led' irrationality that he so despises in the world.

The point of this analysis and work was so that in performance I had a solid foundation from which I hope I was able to develop the interpretation so that it came with ease and was not forced. There were some cast changes when we moved this production from the tour to The Other Place. Most importantly for me Dan Day-Lewis left and Simon Templeman took over as Romeo with only two weeks' rehearsal. This could have been a massive trauma for me, but luckily Simon knew both the production (having played Tybalt on the tour) and me well, as we had joined the RSC at the same time and done many plays together. He grasped his opportunity with relish. The Other Place itself is a much more intimate theatre than the average sports hall of the tour. Technically this led to a greater variety and subtlety of inflection, as less effort is required simply to command the attention of the audience. Perhaps there was the loss of a certain barn-storming vigour that was present on the tour; but for those of us who went on to Stratford, the tour had unified us into a close ensemble, and given us a sense of ourselves that fed our other work there.

Juliet in
Romeo and Juliet
NIAMH CUSACK

N IAMH CUSACK played Juliet in Michael Bogdanov's production of *Romeo and Juliet* at Stratford in 1986 and at the Barbican in 1987. In the preceding season, her first with the RSC, she played Desdemona in *Othello*. Other roles for the RSC have been in *Mary, After the Queen, The Art of Success*, and *Country Dancing*. Earlier work includes roles in *A Woman of No Importance* and *Three Sisters*, as well as a career as a professional flautist.

My mother and both my sisters had played Juliet, but I hardly knew the play when I came to the role for the RSC. I had seen it once, when I was very young, and remembered that I thought it a rather boring play with everyone killing themselves, and I didn't see the point of it all. And so, although a lot of people said that I would make a 'lovely Juliet', that I had the right youthful quality, I had no aspirations to play the part and had the idea, though I hadn't actually read the play, that she was rather a wet. But just a little before starting on Desdemona in Terry Hands's RSC production of *Othello*, I did a scene from *Romeo and Juliet* for a schools television broadcast. Reading the play carefully at the age of twenty-four, when I had just started, as an actress, to explore Shakespeare, I found it wonderful, and my dearest wish from that time was to play Juliet.

The decision to open the 1986 Stratford season with *Romeo and Juliet* was taken late. Though I was already playing Desdemona I was still required to audition for the role, partly because Michael Bogdanov, the director, had never seen my work, but more particularly because he wanted to cast Romeo and Juliet together, as a pair. So after auditioning me alone, I worked on all the scenes with Sean Bean and only after that did Michael decide that we complemented each other appropriately and offer us the parts. The play only works if the balance of the relationship between Romeo and Juliet convinces an audience that they are immediately and irresistibly in love with each other. My Juliet could not exist as it is without

18   Niamh Cusack as Juliet with Romeo (Sean Bean), 1986

Sean Bean's Romeo; I see our relationship, above all in the balcony scene, through him. These are two very different people, both passionate, but he impetuous and wilder, her passion tempered with a practicality that is almost, but not quite, sensible. This richness, this capacity for lateral thinking in her, can only be shown in contrast to Romeo; he is more immature (though perhaps a little older) than her, and it is partly his impetuosity that she falls in love with. I feel that the Romeo I play against serves my Juliet one hundred per cent in the vulnerability and total commitment of his playing of a young boy in love. We meet only five times in the play and if the audience doesn't believe utterly in our love then the whole thing is a waste of time. Juliet's entire development through the play is as a result of what happens between them; at each stage the relationship opens up further and becomes deeper and more consolidated. To explore that requires the confidence that Sean Bean's Romeo gives me.

To move from Desdemona to Juliet was to move from a reactive to an active role. I think that Juliet is considerably younger than Desdemona, but in her play she is the active agent, the person who does everything and who motors the play, particularly in an emotional sense. She is the one who gets things moving all the time, and (before the casting) I wasn't sure that I was regarded by the RSC as this kind of actress. It is a generalization, but there is a sense in which companies divide their actresses into those who do the acting and those who are there to make the stage look pretty. To be cast as Juliet was thus reassuring: it is a big part and it was opening the season, and I told myself they couldn't possibly be risking anyone they thought might be a weak link, for if the Juliet fails there is little point in doing the play. So at first it was very reassuring to be cast – until I began to wonder 'O my God, how am I going to do it?', and to study the part more fully and to see the depth of Juliet's character and how multi-dimensional she is. In the audition I had gone for one aspect of the character, but in the months of rehearsal and playing I have come to realize that there are so many sides to her. One aspect, for example, that emerged only later is the joyous side of her personality at the beginning. I was rather afraid of that at first, in case it should diminish the tragic ending, but of course the more you go for the early joy, the more powerful is the contrasting impact of the final tragedy.

We knew from the beginning that the play would be set in 1986, and Michael was always very clear and open about where the production was going. At first I was a little put off, having come from the long flowing dresses of the Terry Hands *Othello*. But though modern, it was still to be set in Italy, and I wondered where the conflict between the families would come from – why not Northern Ireland, or Israel, or Lebanon. Michael was very firm, however, that the play was set in Italy and that there was no getting away from that. My father, Capulet, was to be presented as a competitive, parvenu businessman, anxious for Juliet to marry Paris as a seal of social respectability. We had the idea that the Montagues were also posher than the Capulets, rather aristocratic but on the way down. The idea of marriage between impoverished aristocracy and the wealthy middle class is perfectly acceptable in Elizabethan terms, of course, and though the motorbikes and the sports car and all the determined trappings of the 1986 setting were picked on by the critics, I do not think that the director ever had any fundamental difficulty in reconciling his concept to what is there in the text. Certainly he was always ready to work closely on the language with us and to suggest readings if we found difficulties. The production was unusual, in my experience, in the contribution of the assistant director Jude Kelly, who worked closely with Michael throughout and did marvellously detailed work on characterization, even in the minor roles. All through rehearsals there was a sense of freedom of exploration of character within the firmly drawn parameters of the production, a willingness on the part of the director to consider the restoration of lines which he had cut, or to discuss any idea openly in front of the company. All this, I think, gave the production an impetus and vitality which have made it immensely invigorating to work in.

At first I took a long time to get used to the fact that, though this was 1986, I couldn't just go out on my own to talk to Romeo, or that we couldn't get on a plane and fly to New Zealand together. In rehearsal one day I think I mentally changed the word 'banished' to 'exiled' and began to find it easier to make the leap: if someone is exiled one can't just follow them, there would be police and legal restrictions. At the beginning, too, I used to wonder about the subservience of Juliet: why, in 1986, should she not be free to make her own choices. But the parallel of the upper classes in present-day England – the marriage market, even the vetting of Lady Diana – helped here. And to the idea that a 1986 Juliet might just telephone for a car to take her to Mantua while the Juliet of the play even has to get permission to go to the Friar, I began to imagine that her father, a wealthy businessman in that claustrophobic atmosphere, would have the telephone tapped and his daughter would live in constant danger of being kidnapped, so that if she made a move his guards would be straight after her. Gradually I came to terms with the modern setting.

The setting was important in establishing Juliet's situation and relationships at the beginning of the play. As the production developed I played the first scene to show Juliet more and more obviously enjoying the Nurse, naively not seeing through her, or through her mother. Only later will that knowledge come and then she will act on it with total integrity to herself. What is marvellous is that the more you can let her be as naive and young as she is and as close to the Nurse as she can possibly get, the more heartrending it is when she discovers that the Nurse has no comprehension of what she is like inside or what her values are. Juliet, this production suggests, has no relationship with her mother. The sophistication, the clothes, the *Dynasty*-like figure, the ill-concealed affair Lady Capulet is having with Tybalt, are all outside Juliet's area of questioning. She has been brought up in this environment and knows no other; protected but without friends; no one to go out to meet on the piazza, no motor-scooter like all the boys seem to have; no one to compare notes with. A limo takes her here, there, and everywhere; life is organized for her and very sheltered. She has no reason to be unhappy, so she does not question whether she is happy or not. She is an only child who talks to things, to objects, as if they were people. She has a rich imagination and she sees all manner of things; when she looks at the sky she doesn't just see the sky – there's a world peopled with lives up there. To think of her in this way helps me to find the youthfulness of the part. She has the ability to be self-sufficient – you realize that as the play goes on – but here, as the play begins, she seems firmly set in her friendship with the Nurse. Later we discover that she will have little trouble in withdrawing from that apparent reliance; she needs the Nurse rather less than Romeo needs the Friar. Romeo is not as mature as she is and always needs someone to give him a sense of direction. Even at the end, as he defies the stars and decides to take his own life, he is still doing it because he is thinking of her. Juliet has a greater sense of reliance on herself and confidence in her own point of view.

I felt this increasingly as we worked on the opening scene. Her reply to the suggestion that she should marry Paris is guarded and ambiguous; she is covering herself. 'I'll do my best' is what she seems to say to her mother, but she doesn't commit herself. This is someone who has learned to protect herself, not in any defensive or neurotic way, but quite openly. She looks at her mother and thinks 'I won't be like that'; there is no problem about it, no rebellion, no 'I can't bear her clothes, or her values', but something quite simple and therefore strong. She is obviously taking in what she sees, but she isn't influenced by all that's around her and keeps her own unique sense of what is right and wrong. This was something I felt from very early in rehearsals – that Juliet is a really special spirit, in another world from everyone else. Being innocent is not the fashion in today's cynical society and I didn't want her to be naive or to be laughed at. So I tried to find a sense of her covering herself well in that first careful response to her mother: 'I'll look to like, if looking liking move', but then, even more carefully: 'But no more deep will I endart mine eye / Than your consent gives strength to make it fly' (1.3.96–9). 'I'll certainly try to like the look of him', she says, 'but obviously I won't go any further than you would wish me to.' It's terribly diplomatic and at first I rehearsed it as if she knew exactly what her mother was up to and what a grabbing, immoral woman she is, but later I felt very firmly that Juliet does not think in that way. How do you speak to your mother, who is not like your nurse, who is not a stranger, but who doesn't speak to you very often? That sort of language has got to come from obedience and it's got to be polite. There is no need, I discovered, to play her reply 'It is an honour that I dream not of' coldly, as if she is deliberately hiding herself; there is no need to protect the character from the audience (Shakespeare can do that well enough if the need arises). The reply comes naturally from Juliet's innocence and self-sufficiency. One does not have to present modern teenage rebelliousness, or boredom with the Nurse's stories, or to look for a 'spoiled brat' quality. Juliet is unique, and the 1986 setting, or any other setting, leaves the performer still trying to represent that unique spirit.

Juliet is awakened from her state of apparent contentment and self-possession by the meeting with Romeo. There is a marvellous flirtatiousness about that first sonnet they speak together, but she is covering, not letting herself go too much, though she is obviously feeling enormous passion for him, and is almost overwhelmed by the feeling. Never before has she met anyone so in tune with her as to be able to exchange lines with her in a sonnet, who so exactly complements her, anyone with whom she doesn't have to compromise. She looks at him and thinks 'My God, this is incredible', and it is more so when she talks to him and the feeling is continued. Though they talk the same language they are not saying quite the same things: she is obviously taking her part in the flirtation, but she manages ostensibly to talk about lips being used for prayer. She tries to be careful while all he can do is think 'give us a kiss'. Left alone afterwards she passionately vows that she would rather die than have anyone else. Her choice of words is unconsciously ironic: 'If he be married, my grave is like to prove my wedding bed' (1.5.135). Not until after he has gone and she has learned that he is a Montague does she decide that she must do something to make sure that she sees this man again. It is this realization of who he is that makes her see for the first time that she is caged. That is how I feel when I go up onto that balcony at the end of the ball scene and the Nurse tells me that all the guests have left and I know that he has gone too. All I want to do is to run out of the gate after him, and I can't, and it's the first time I realize that there are guards and high walls and that I can't actually go out at two o'clock in the morning looking for this man. And the awful thing is that he is caged too, because if I turned up on the Montague doorstep, a Capulet, at best they would send me back home in my limo, at worst kill me or kidnap me as a hostage. So this is the moment that I realize I am imprisoned in the environment I have been brought up in. As I stand there on the balcony, I challenge the Capulet credo of 'Hate all Montagues'.

Then he arrives, and the first feeling is just joy. But Juliet is still a little inhibited, I feel (though she doesn't actually say so), by what her family is and by the problem of reconciling her love and her family commitment. When she thinks he is not there she can say that she will give up everything for him; when he appears and they start talking, and talking, about love, she gets, not second thoughts exactly, but a sense of the need to try to be sensible. 'The orchard walls are high and hard to climb', she says, and laughs at the passionate earnestness of his reply: 'With love's light wings did I o'er-perch these walls' (2.2.63, 66). We haven't seen her sense of humour before, but here it comes over strongly. What is marvellous about the balcony scene is that it shows two very real people and you can imagine them actually growing old together and having grandchildren. They complement each other perfectly, Romeo a little immature and reckless, a bit over the top, dreaming of flying to the moon, while she is trying to be sensible and saying well, if you really do love me, let's get married. She is her parents' daughter in this, trying to be practical, trying to think of all the angles – the characteristics that will later make her capable of lying in order to protect her love. Her practical determination emerges most clearly when she returns to the balcony after her brief exit. Suddenly she seems to realize that she has to make an absolute decision to leave the world she has been brought up in and marry the man she loves. To explain this new mood when she returns I imagine that when she goes off to have that quick word with the Nurse, pressure must be put on her about the marriage to Paris; this would at least explain the complete change in tone, speed, and rhythm when she comes back and becomes so urgent in her talk of marriage to Romeo. Even when she makes this choice, however, she cannot realize what is going to happen; how could she, since it is only the death of Tybalt that changes everything? If she had been allowed more time to think she would presumably have confronted her family with the *fait accompli* after her marriage to Romeo; and she must still hope here that a final, total break will not be necessary.

Juliet is, I think, consistently positive about the relationship. From the beginning right up to the moment when she discovers Romeo dead, she is hopeful, willing their love to work. Her foreboding remarks – 'my grave is like to prove my wedding bed', 'I have no joy in this contract tonight', etc. – come from a kind of sixth sense, below conscious thought. They are remarks for the audience to absorb, like Romeo's as he enters the Capulet ball, but they have no effect on the positive attitude they both take to the relationship. Even when she says goodbye to him in the dawn scene and sees him as 'one dead in the bottom of a tomb' there is no conscious sense of doom. I do not think she is at this point aware that they could actually kill themselves; she hasn't been driven to that yet. It is the shock of the imminence of the planned marriage to Paris, when she thought she had more time, that begins to bring these things to the surface, though even then her reaction 'God I'd rather die than do that' is a very human one of a kind that we rarely expect to have to take literally – that is the brilliance of it. To play Juliet as if she is conscious of the inevitability of tragedy is the same thing as to play her wisely aware of all the faults of the society she lives in: if you do this too soon you have nowhere to go, and if she is not full of hope and promise then there is much less sense of tragedy at the end. It is for the audience alone to savour the fact that she really is foretelling the future, though even they, I think, often come to the play over-conscious of its ending and of the idea of the 'star-crossed' lovers; I hope our production surprises them sometimes with the positiveness and energy of its early stages. Juliet certainly does not think of herself as 'star-crossed'; she makes her choices quite freely and her choices bring her to where she finishes.

I have to say, therefore, that omitting the prologue so as not to close down the options, and moving it to the end as our production does, seems to me a very good idea – fortunately, for this was something about which Michael Bogdanov was immovable. He had decided absolutely on the shape of the play, and though he was often flexible if one fought for lines which had been cut, he was completely firm in what he wanted for the structure and in his desire to make a statement about a society and about that society's method of mourning the only worthwhile thing in it. Treating the play's last moments as a news conference, with the prologue given by the Duke at the end as a sort of press release, and the reconciliation of the families blatantly posed for the cameras, is to refuse to soften the play, as Shakespeare rather tends to, in its finale. It seems to me to make the play much more real for the audience, something much more like real life. We also cut Friar Laurence's long recapitulation, again with the idea of not allowing the audience to find comfort in distancing themselves from the situation through a long passage of narrative.

But to return to Juliet's progress through the play: in the balcony scene her love seems complete. We see her next in the bright light of day – 'The clock struck nine when I did send the Nurse' (2.5.1) – and things are not quite the same as they seemed in the preceding night. That odd sense of uncertainty about first being in love has taken over. Not until she is married will Juliet feel secure at the end of the journey of courtship; here the 'if' of the balcony scene's 'If that thy bent of love be honourable' is dominant. Whenever you fall in love you are never sure of the other person at the beginning, and this uncertainty and impatience in Juliet are all taken out on the Nurse. She is not yet sure of Romeo, or of her destiny; not until the wedding scene at Laurence's chapel will she be at peace. Every scene of the play is part of a developing story. The balcony scene doesn't finally consolidate their love: the ups and downs and uncertainties continue and here now at midday she wonders why the Nurse has taken 'three long hours' to return; could it be that he didn't turn up, that he got caught by his family; her imagination is running riot.

The wedding scene brings confidence and peace and we next see her anticipating the consummation of their love: 'Gallop apace, you fiery-footed steeds' (3.2.1). The richness of texture of that speech is extraordinary. I ask night, gentle night, loving night, passionate night, every sort of night, to give Romeo to me. I try every angle on night, so as to make that little pact: give him to me, so that he can come to me, so that I can have him, and then 'when I shall die' you can have him – 'take him, and cut him out in little stars'. My first reading of the word *die* here is the sexual one: the white of the stars, and his body in white, and the white of him ejaculating inside me, and the cutting up in little white stars, linking, at that pervasively unconscious level of foreboding, with the idea of spiritual death, which immediately afterwards breaks into the scene in reality with the news of the death of Tybalt.

The next phase of the play is the one where Juliet really grows up. When she discovers that Romeo has killed her cousin and then been banished she has to come to terms with where her loyalties lie. I always feel that she understands what commitment and depth of love are in this scene; she comes to terms with the idea of being a wife, and with the responsibility of it, as she makes herself face up to the fact that being married to someone means that you stand by him even if he has killed someone you love. That is what is implied in the keeping of marriage vows, and this is where she becomes a wife rather than a girl playing at being a wife. In the first phase of the play it is possible to think of her love for Romeo, though huge and total, as adolescent, but from this moment on she is a woman embracing the role of wife, facing its truth, taking part in it, inhabiting it. This scene is the turning point for Juliet, the realization that a wife's love must come on top of all other loves and that it can give her the strength to do everything that she now has to do.

She is alone now, and that loneliness is pointed by the final break with the Nurse. When the Nurse advises her to marry Paris she thinks she is still talking to a little girl; she hasn't realized that she is talking to a woman who has made a lifelong commitment to Romeo. The effect of the Nurse's advice is in fact to confirm Juliet in that commitment, not to unsettle her in the least. She has made the decision about where her loyalties lie in the scene when she learns of Tybalt's death, and now to hear the Nurse flippantly describing Romeo as a dishclout makes the decision easier and clearer for her, even though breaking with the Nurse means cutting away something that is very deep in her. If the Nurse had tried to be more understanding and persuasive – 'I know Romeo is a lovely man, but you've got to do this, this is the only way, maybe we can find a way round it afterwards' – it might have been more difficult, but the fact that she belittles Romeo makes the decision stark and the break complete. It tears Juliet's heart for a second that this woman, who she thought loved her and understood her, can say these things, but once she hears them there is no love any more, for you can't love someone whose values are so far away from your own and who, it is suddenly clear, doesn't really understand what love is: 'Ancient damnation!' (3.5.235).

She is now quite alone, the Nurse and her parents irrelevant. It is easy to come on and lie to them after her visit to the Friar, because they now mean nothing to me. She has hardened, at least externally, covering her inner vulnerability with an ice cold manner that makes her uncompromising with the Friar, capable of lying quite easily, quite simply, to her parents about the plan for immediate marriage to Paris. There is always the knife if the potion doesn't work.

The grim determination of Juliet's superficial mood when she goes to

Friar Laurence covers inner desperation. She turns to Laurence because there is nowhere else to go. Obviously she does not have the same depth of relationship with him as does Romeo. For her he is the local padre who has christened, married, and buried all the families she knows. He has probably prepared her for her first communion, but the relationship is not at all like Laurence's with Romeo who would for years have been a member of his local boys' football team. For Romeo he is a close confidant, someone he trusts absolutely to keep a secret, even a secret marriage. There are two people who know of that marriage, the Nurse and the Friar. When the

19   Juliet with her Nurse (Dilys Laye) and her parents

Nurse turns out to be a dud card, Juliet must go to the Friar, not because she trusts him especially, but because he represents the last hope of escape and will himself get into deep water if he doesn't find that way out. But Laurence does not really know her and I think it really shakes him when she shows the strength of her commitment to Romeo in pulling that knife. At one time, before the production opened, we were rehearsing a mimed scene in which I took the knife from my father's desk. It is realistic to assume that such a man as the Capulet of this production would have a gun to protect himself, and perhaps a knife too, so that when I say 'If all else fail, myself have power to die' I do know that there is a weapon in the house that I can use. We toyed with the idea of a gun, in keeping with our modern setting, but concluded that a knife is much more graphic and pulling it out, with the threat of slitting your throat, much more disturbing.

As she arrives at Friar Laurence's cell, Juliet has to endure a conversation with Paris. The emotional strain of having to exchange courtesies with this flirtatious young man when all she wants to do is to get on with her appeal to the Friar, makes this a difficult moment for her. To be close to him, then to be kissed by him, is repulsive and the feeling of being caged in is made even stronger by the meeting. Whatever she felt about being in the same house with those people, parents and nurse, who have no idea what she is feeling inside, is intensified by this meeting with the man who will keep her in that kind of life. Everything he says is possessive of her at a moment when she is desperately trying to escape from the nightmare of the world she has been brought up in and lives in. The meeting with Paris is, I think, the final straw that makes it easy for her to pull the knife and to be so vicious about it, so that once again she drives the action forward, forcing Friar Laurence to think of something.

Whether Juliet believes at once in the Friar's remedy is hardly the question. She is desperate, a drowning woman, and she will grab at anything that has a faint hope about it, anything that might save her marriage. She has had nothing but negatives for the past few hours and here is the Friar talking positively, suggesting that there may be a way out. And she will take any way out that's offered – that, certainly, is how I want to play the scene. The only thing that scares her is the idea of the tomb, right here at its first mention, well before the soliloquy about it. What is odd is that she has just said that she'll do anything, even lie with dead and rotting bones, and he calls her bluff and immediately she starts to wonder 'can I do this?'. That is her real fear, waking up with the dead, a young girl surrounded by dead bodies and rotting limbs. The Friar's insistence that

that is what she is going to have to do sends her back home with a couple of hours to think about it and then, when the Nurse and her mother go out, Juliet is left alone with that bottle, confronting death and the unknown.

We begin this scene with Juliet playing the flute. Michael Bogdanov is like a fond parent who likes all his children to be shown off at their best, and very early on he had decided that Michael Kitchen was going to play his guitar and Hugh Quarshie his saxophone, and I knew that he knew that I could play the flute. I was therefore dreading the moment when he would say 'why don't you play the flute for a bit in the middle of the balcony scene?' So I was well armed against that idea, but as we talked about the vial speech we wondered how we might set it and I said that I thought she would be completely removed from the rest of the household's concerns, presumably in her bedroom. Michael felt that we needed to start the scene in some way that would give a sense of her commitment to Romeo and of her being part of his world and no one else's any longer. And so came the idea of her playing the flute, which I agreed to so long as I could choose the piece, because I knew immediately that the right piece was Debussy's 'Syrinx', which is so haunting and so utterly different from all the other modern music in the production. The music is her escape to another world, but it doesn't seem at all strange to her parents, or to the Nurse, that she should play her flute, and it reinforces the idea of her being a lonely girl, as she has been all through the play, the sort of girl often alone, who might well play a good deal of music, read a lot, and dream. So, having resisted the idea in anticipation, the flute-playing at this moment of loneliness now seems to me right, an appropriate prelude to the speech in which she faces the ordeal of swallowing the Friar's potion.

When I began work on the role I was not aware that that speech was regarded as notoriously difficult – and that, no doubt, is a very good thing. We didn't rehearse it until quite late and when we started (partly, I suppose, because my training is as a musician) I was already seeing it as a musical shape. This is my usual habit, to see just the basic outline, and the crescendos and diminuendos, but to have difficulty in finding the detail. I worked alone with the director on the speech and he was very good in encouraging me to look for one idea, deal with that, and then go on to the next one. My feeling was that Juliet actually had to reach a point of madness in order to take that potion. The problem is to move towards that, but to make the ideas and images and fears along the way fully vivid and theatrical. At the beginning I don't think I was finding the reality of the speech; I was just playing the individual images, without showing where they came from or the effect they were having on me. I gradually discovered the need to take it apart more, and to play it more simply, like a little girl telling herself a story, but a wild and frightening story. This approach has been a great help for me; it simplifies the speech and stops me from attacking the audience too much with it. I start off with a tiny fear and it just gets bigger and bigger. One must be totally committed to each fear in turn, to the horrible images that keep rolling out. They are all horrible images and they don't necessarily come in any particular order; one thing is really revolting and then, my God, there is another, and so on. To play the speech a little more as a terrified child has certainly helped me to find more colour in it. The extraordinary thing about this terrified child, this girl of fourteen, is the speed with which she achieves the maturity to make the big choices and decisions and to take responsibility for them. That she is young in years in the world does not mean that she is not wise or that she lacks great strength, as this speech makes clear. From the cheerful, happy, positive decision-making of the balcony scene, we have moved to this terrifying decision to swallow the bottle of whatever it is the Friar has given her.

Juliet's last scene is in the tomb which she has here so vividly imagined. The first few seconds of waking up and believing it has all worked out must be played for all their happiness. The poison did not kill me, everything has gone according to plan, there is the Friar, and I am where I am supposed to be – all this, I think, has to be suggested in those moments though you have only just woken up and are a little bit dozy. Then you turn and see the man whom you last saw looking up at you so alive and full of love lying there dead, and you know that he can't see you, that he can never see you again, that he can't feel you though you are actually together, and there is nothing that you can do ever to wake him. In order to take the potion Juliet has had to kill every other feeling she has ever had for other people. It is for Romeo that she takes the potion: 'Romeo! Here's drink – I drink to thee.' Now she discovers the man for whose love she did that lying dead beside her and it is a very simple decision to kill herself. There is no life now, the only life you ever had is dead; my whole motor through the play has been him, and my love for him. In the balcony scene I suddenly realized that there are parts of me that have never lived, never vibrated or breathed, and then I met him and we had that wonderful time talking to each other, and so I can never go back to what I was. There is no choice here now; real life is with him and to see him dead is to see myself dead. It is as simple as that and I don't even hear the Friar, with his last little urgent scheme. I look at Romeo and there is no choice. For part of the run of our production Romeo, in keeping with our modern setting, had killed himself by injecting poison through a hypodermic needle; for me, earlier, we had toyed with the idea of a gun to pull on the Friar in my desperate search for an escape; but here at the end there was never any doubt. The moment is simple, brief; there is no savouring of it, no making the dreadful grief and loss any deeper than it is. Just get it over with, finish, numb: 'This is thy sheath; there rust, and let me die.'

Ophelia in
Hamlet

FRANCES BARBER

FRANCES BARBER played Ophelia in Ron Daniels's production of *Hamlet* in Stratford in 1984 and at the Barbican the following year. In the same season, her first with the RSC, she played the title role in Pam Gems's *Camille*, which later transferred to the West End, and Jaquenetta in *Love's Labour's Lost*. Television work includes Mike Leigh's *Home Sweet Home* and Doug Lucie's *Hard Feelings* and films *Zed and Two Noughts*, *Prick up Your Ears* and *Sammy and Rosie Get Laid*. Her most recent RSC role was in *The Dead Monkey* (London, The Pit) in 1987.

The difference between reading a completely new play for the first time, and reading one of the most famous plays in literature with a view to acting one of the most famous tragic heroines, became clear to me two years ago in Stratford. In an attempt to make the character your own, there is a great temptation to invent an entirely new characteristic 'hidden' in the text. Any aspect of the character you may hit upon as being innovatory to your final reading has invariably been discovered, discussed, and updated in the wealth of literary criticism surrounding the play.

On hearing I was to tackle this role, I had a fairly traditional image of Ophelia in my mind. The obedient young girl whose sense of self is defined by the court in which she lives, and hence the men around her, is used as an instrument of political machinations, and ends up hysterical. This invariably took on a visual image of nightgowns and flowers. I had seen the play only once, at the Royal Court when Jonathan Pryce did his famous 'double-act' of conjuring up Hamlet's ghost from the pit of his stomach. Harriet Walter – an actress I greatly admire – had played Ophelia, which dispelled any traditional images of the weak, stupid girl which may have been lurking in the minds of the audience. I carried this memory with me for many weeks preparing for the same role.

After wading through essays, articles, and footnotes on the meaning of the mad scenes, her attitude to the Prince, her function in the play, from

Leavis to Kott, I decided to abandon any early idea I may have had of finding an 'Alternative Ophelia' for the sake of being different. I had no real fear that I was going to be asked to play her in a way I found repugnant. You learn very early on as an actress that you are nearly always cast because of certain qualities you may possess – or at any rate certain qualities a director thinks you are particularly good at conveying. Being weak is not one of my strengths.

Some actors build ideas of their characterisation outside the rehearsal room and enter that space fully armed with argument and justification of their interpretations. This particular approach I had never attempted before, preferring to work from scratch on a part, with other actors offering ideas and exploring various dead-ends together. But because this was my Shakespearean debut, I felt compelled to arrive on Day One with some idea of how I wished to tackle the role. So, abandoning the critics, I set about reading the play again and again, jotting down anything I felt personally drawn to in the character on the page.

The characteristic that constantly reappears in all Shakespeare's women

20   Frances Barber as Ophelia with Hamlet (Roger Rees), 1984

is their intelligence. The very way they speak, the language they use, is in every way as illuminating as his male characters, and they usually present a logical point of view to help provide a balance, to fill out the areas of feminine sensibilities that some of his men often lack. My initial impressions of Ophelia, however, led me to suspect that I would find her an exception to this, or at any rate not appear as 'complete' as some of his women generally are. The first thing that struck me was quite the reverse. She is acutely intelligent and highly perceptive. Because of her position at court she has to choose her words even more carefully than, say, Miranda or Juliet. She recognises the potential repercussions of Hamlet's madness before anyone else in the play; albeit she is powerless to prevent them. My thoughts then ran to why she is therefore traditionally seen in such an ineffective passive capacity, and I discovered that rather than being an extension of Hamlet's character, she actually presents the female counterpart and counterpoint to him. She provides the feminine qualities lacking in his sensibilities. Shakespeare uses her innocence and naiveté to illustrate this imbalance and highlight its consequences; the destruction of a potent feminine force, caught up in a male-dominated power struggle. However thin on paper, her function in the play is therefore vital: to suggest to the audience an alternative set of events, very much in the 'if only' tradition. I had never underestimated the challenge of creating Ophelia; what I hadn't taken into consideration was how very much more there was to her than a couple of mad scenes. These observations formed the yardstick by which any further discoveries I was to make about her were to be measured, and ironically I too became one of those actors armed with justification for my characterisation on entering the rehearsal room.

On first discussing the part with the director, Ron Daniels, I excitedly told him of my discoveries:
'She's full of humour and wit and intelligence, she's strong, courageous, emotionally open. She shows her independence when she gives Hamlet his "remembrances" back, she stands up to her father, she . . .'
'Frankie, you *can't* play her as a feminist, it's not in the text.'
'Oh but it is, Ron, oh but it is.' (I had done my justification research rather thoroughly.)
'Why does she go mad then?'
'Because she's the only person in the play who sees what's going on.'
'And?'
'And she's full of guilt for not having been able to prevent it.'
'And?'

'And she's full of remorse for her father's death.'

'And?'

'And she blames herself for Hamlet's prejudice against women.'

'And?'

'And she's guilt-ridden, Ron! She's utterly guilt-ridden, like every woman I know; and she's culpable to a point because she knew Claudius and Polonius were spying on Hamlet but she didn't warn him. And she knows he's physically attracted to her and she sort of encourages it.'

'What?'

'Well I think she does' (my armoury of qualification in the text was beginning to run a bit thin).

Stubbornly refusing to be blown about by argument or threat, I entered those initial days of rehearsal with the notion that the play we were embarking upon was really called 'Ophelia and her Downfall'. I was intent upon discovering a way of playing her that revealed the masculine as well as the feminine qualities Hamlet lacked. This even went as far as a suggestion that she should first be seen actually fighting Laertes on his departure as a swordswoman every bit as accomplished as her brother. This idea was abandoned very early on, much to the relief of a rather shocked Ron Daniels, when we discovered that the women's costumes were possibly the most unsuitable garments ever designed from which to hang and whip out an RSC sword. Besides which, the text does provide enough information to convey Ophelia's spirit, without resorting to a physical boxing match. I had been convinced.

Ron wished to explore three worlds of cosmic, political and domestic implications in the text. The rehearsal process developed along the lines of exploring each scene with these three factors in isolation, and then finding ways in which they converged. The domestic situation of the Polonius family is in a way wholly defined by the political ramifications of Polonius's ambition at court. Consequently it is no ordinary family difference of opinion when her brother and father advise her to have nothing more to do with Hamlet. Ron encouraged Frank Middlemass to play Polonius as a very strict father and a devious political operator. This gave me an opportunity to kick against the 'kind old dad' image, suggesting more of a confrontation in the scene. In the previous wedding scene I had deliberately chosen to look at Hamlet as often as I could, concerned as to the effect the marriage had upon him. This had not gone unnoticed by Laertes and Polonius, so the advice levelled at her here comes as no surprise. In fact we decided that Polonius had probably instructed his son to work on her before his departure. I therefore began the scene being almost evasive in my replies, but still truthfully not knowing 'What I should think.' As this enrages Polonius, her resolve that Hamlet has behaved honourably becomes strengthened during the scene, not weakened. In the early days of rehearsal, when I did not know my lines, Frank and I played the scene avoiding eye-contact until the final order forbidding her ever to see Hamlet again, at which point I turned round in full flight ready to defend the Prince's intentions, shouting 'line!' to the prompt corner as I had dried. 'I shall obey, my Lord', came the reply; but I had physically rounded on Polonius in such a way that to deliver the line in any way other than defiantly became impossible. I continued this form of attack, breaking into Frank's next line as I believed he had finished, to which he barked 'Look to't I charge you!' Ron liked the inversion of the lines at this point, so my final acquiescence came only after several attempted interruptions; the scene ending with 'Come your ways!' rather like an exasperated father trying to tame his wild daughter. This was a very early reading of the scene, and it underwent some softening of the edges as the rehearsals continued, but the basic tone of the scene never altered. It was an attempt to convey Ophelia's trust in Hamlet, despite all the warnings against him by the only other men in her life. As my initial turning on Polonius had been so fierce, it prompted Frank to remark, 'I'm rather glad you decided not to have that sword, darling, or I really wonder whether poor old dad would have had any chance of continuing the play.'

This glimpse of independence actually helped me approach some of the more 'difficult' scenes that follow. It gave me an idea of how to tackle the scene in which Ophelia reports Hamlet's appearance to her in her rooms. I could never understand why she runs to tell Polonius of her premonition, aside from the obvious fact that since her brother's departure he is the only person with whom she has any connection. As I played the preceding scene emphasising her trust in Hamlet, it seemed unlikely to me that she would reveal her suspicions of his behaviour so soon afterwards. After many dismal attempts at justifying her search for her father because of her deep fear and concern for the Prince, I came to the conclusion that she wasn't seeking out Polonius after all, but stumbles upon him accidentally, relieved to be able to share with someone the dark fears forming in her mind. The 'cosmic' and political implications of Hamlet's behaviour over-ride the domestic circumstances in which she finds herself, making her description a discovery, her first in the spiral of her perceptions up to the end of the play scene. Because I played her account of Hamlet's actions as the beginnings of her realisation, Polonius's 'come, go we to the king' comes as something of a shock to her. I tried to convey that at this point she has second thoughts about divulging so much information, and consequently in the scene with Rosencrantz and Guildenstern I felt it useful to continue this line of thought, implying her disquiet at being party to some sort of trap set for Hamlet; she realises they are working for Claudius, when she has presumably heard they are Hamlet's friends. As the two men withdrew from the scene, I stared after them, causing one of them to look back to see this, and tell his companion.

Because Gertrude is unhappy about using Ophelia to confront her son, it is the only opportunity to show any connection the women may have – and here began an ongoing disagreement between Ron and me as to how I delivered the line 'Madam, I wish it may.' I emphasised the 'I', causing the director to groan each time the scene was played. I was desperate to indicate that the only reason she had agreed to participate in the encounter set up by Polonius was to help Hamlet, hence *I* wish it may reassemble his wandering mind, as well as the queen.

When we began rehearsing the nunnery scene, Roger Rees established early on that he didn't want to play the accusations levelled at Ophelia because he realises that Claudius and Polonius are listening, but rather be taken aback at his own desire for this woman, whom he regards as a 'wanton sinner', as a result of his mother's adultery. Here was an opportunity to work on the 'if only' theme; particularly as the scene was to be played as if they are truly alone. There were two main ingredients I wished to communicate, her culpability and her premonition. The remembrances I was handed as a rehearsal prop was a locket on a chain that I wore around my neck. Maria Bjornson, the designer, had elected to dress the whole court in grey for the first half of the play. My costume had the effect of an almost straight-laced Victorian affair, with a very high neck, buttoned up to the chin. Undoing the neck of the dress only to the throat, to reveal the token, produced an effect of 'innocent guile'. Hamlet finds this an irresistible sexual provocation, resulting in a passionate embrace that Ophelia responds to. Roger wanted to show Hamlet's disgust at his own ardour, and did so by physically rejecting me, throwing me about the stage and finally to the floor. He even went as far in one rehearsal as slapping my face (which gesture unfortunately remained for the 150 or so performances of the play). As I had decided that Ophelia should stand up to Hamlet in the scene, using emphasis on the way she actually addresses him – 'My Lord', 'How does your honour', 'Good my Lord', and, when rebuked, 'My honour'd lord', with only the slightest hint of indignation – her use of 'for to the noble mind' contrasts with her formal addresses, implying a former intimacy and suggesting she in some way disapproves of his strange behaviour. As the scene proceeds and Hamlet becomes even more violent towards her, Roger clasped my face, spitting out all his accusations against women directly at her, implying that women, and particularly herself, are the direct cause of his troubled mind. Each of these accusations became pointers later to her feelings of guilt when we see her in the mad scenes. By the time we reach her lament for his reason ('blasted with ecstasy'), I wanted to convey not only her horror as she realises the consequences of this, but also to suggest that she is in some way to blame. I looked down to see the neck of the dress open, and guiltily buttoned it up as I exited.

As the rehearsals progressed and each day a clearer picture of the sort of woman I wished to create began to emerge, I became increasingly worried at the prospect of stepping onto the stage of the Royal Shakespeare Theatre without any formal voice training behind me. I had only recently joined the company to play Marguerite in Pam Gems's version of *Camille*, a modern play despite its traditional source – and in The Other Place, a small studio space, not such a departure from the type of work I had previously spent five years doing. I needed some help.

Cicely Berry introduced me to a whole new area of acting I had never explored before. I had been criticised since joining the Company for my flat vowel sounds. I come from the Midlands and my 'O's and 'A's were a veritable credit to that region of the country. I also discovered that I had a strangulated 'throat' voice; I wasn't using my breathing properly and had very little control over the sound I was producing. None of which boded well for my first attempt at verse speaking. All these defects (as I termed them, not Cis) became vital elements to overcome before I could feel in any way prepared to tackle and do justice to this most famous of roles. As Ophelia lives in the court of the king and queen, is betrothed to the Prince of Denmark, and has a father who is the equivalent of the prime minister, it is unlikely that she would have acquired a 'suburban twang', as one critic had described my voice in *Camille*. Eradicating my flat vowel sounds became something of an obsession that even now hasn't entirely left me.

A session with Cis can be rather like a confessional with your best friend. She occupies a tiny, square-shaped room on the top floor of the Memorial Theatre's maze of corridors, in which she reassures you that anything discussed or divulged there is never to be repeated. Her aim is for you to discover your own potential, allowing you the freedom to use your voice in any way you wish. To achieve this you have to learn how to be as relaxed as possible on stage, taking breaths only where Shakespeare indicates, using the control of your voice to embody the emotions of the verse. The theory of all this was confusing for a novice like myself, but in practice she would lay you down on the floor, blow cigarette smoke all over you, pull your arms, pat your chest, and usually make you laugh until she was sure you were relaxed and she could set about freeing your voice. I spent an hour a day with Cis during those eight weeks or so of rehearsals, learning how to relax, learning how to breathe by filling the back of my lungs with air, storing it, controlling its escape, discovering I had a bigger voice if I used my chest to produce the sound rather than my throat, erasing my flat vowel sounds. And all the time discussing politics, women, women in Shakespeare, punks, pop music, anything that came to mind.

She finally agreed to my request for her to tape some of Ophelia's speeches so that I could practise the vowel sounds that I found most difficult: 'hand, hand, hand'; 'out, out, out'; 'brow, brow, brow'. Cis believes that the vowels are the most important sounds in verse speaking. Shakespeare uses particular words and sounds to guide you through his speeches, indicating speed, urgency, relevance. If you follow his guidelines you will embody the emotion he requires, not artificially invent an emotion on top of the verse. 'O what a noble mind . . .' had been a stumbling block for me for some time; all those descriptions of Hamlet, her already highly charged state at the opening of the speech, her premonition of what is to come, and uppermost in my mind her own feelings of being in some way responsible, took on for me a formidable image of scaling a summit, not to mention all those 'A's, 'O's and 'E's lurking in the text. Cis must have worked on that speech with me over a hundred times. I began to understand for the first time the importance of breath control. Ophelia's perceptions are tumbling out of her in such an urgent state that there is no time to stop for a quick gulp of air to finish off a thought.

Cis pointed out that Shakespeare's other characters that go mad have either rousing speeches like Lear's 'Blow winds', or Lady Macbeth's jagged and brittle 'Out, out, damned spot'. All Ophelia's speeches are soft and rhythmic; they have a fluidity, suggesting things tend to happen to her, because of her position in the political operations around her, and reinforcing her feminine sensibilities. Within this quality there is a dignity and strength, her perceptions are as carefully formed as Hamlet's, but they concentrate on the pathos of the circumstances she finds herself in, not the revenge aspect. Because of her powerlessness to prevent what she sees, it seems inevitable that her mind should break in two; and entirely apposite that when this happens her words should come out in song. The prose in the mad scenes is the only time Ophelia doesn't have to keep to any strict metre or rhythm, as if Shakespeare is suggesting that the actress must find an important contrast in the very way she speaks, when her mind is broken.

My sessions with Cis were often full of wonder and delight at this entirely new set of options open to me, but they were often fraught with frustration bordering on despair that I wouldn't have time to assimilate all this invaluable information coming my way, and of course the persistent anxiety of all those 'hands, hands, hands' hovering in the text. Miraculously, and very near the opening, it did all finally begin to come together. I wasn't aware of waking up one morning and discovering the Road to Damascus; I just carried on taking deep breaths and exhaling 'out, out, out', as often as I could. Arriving at Cis's room one morning requesting the tape of vowel sounds she had reluctantly agreed to make for me (she didn't want to give me line readings), she said 'You don't need it any longer, darling, you've got it.' I was shattered. 'You can't mean it, Cis. I know you don't want to do this for me, but please *hand* it over, or I shall walk *out* of here and never come *back*.' 'There you are,' she replied, 'I told you so.'

By the time I came to rehearse the mad scenes, I had a pretty substantial idea of what I wanted to achieve, but many decisions yet to take as to how to execute these ideas. I had no desire to produce a cabaret of 'mad acting' that had very little to do with what went before, neither did I wish to resort to presenting a poor young girl running round the stage distributing flowers. Whilst watching the rehearsals progressing, I noticed Roger as Hamlet became more lucid and reasonable as his obsessions took him over. He also used particular gestures each time he saw his father's ghost, and he was truly in danger of losing his mind. If I was to follow through my theme of Ophelia as a female counterpart to the Prince, it seemed interesting to incorporate some of Hamlet's gestures into the most inappropriate moments of her own madness, highlighting her then as his female counterpoint. Consequently one of Roger's most striking gestures was that of banging his chest violently after the ghost has appeared to him for the first time, as if his heart truly is breaking.

As I was exploring a way of using my voice as softly as I could, in contrast with the forthright delivery of the earlier scenes, I decided to bang my chest and beat my heart as violently as I could at the most unexpected moment, during the sweetness of the song. This seemed to fit in with the research I had done on 'madness' as we know it today: people are 'certified' if they are likely to do harm to others or to themselves. I wanted to suggest that whilst Hamlet is likely to do harm to others at his most revengeful, Ophelia is capable of doing herself great harm at her most tranquil. Her madness then took on the form of wander-witted regret. As my theme was guilt, I tried to stave off those feelings of blame until they finally explode from within her; 'and thou hadst not come to my bed' (4.5.66) became the springboard for her feelings of her own wickedness. At this point I broke down weeping at the feet of Gertrude, clutching the queen's hand as the only other female involved in the spiral of events, imploring 'all will be well'. The implication of 'we must be patient' was in some ways then a plea for all women: we must hope that our femininity will finally percolate into the male sensibilities. 'To think they would lay him i' the cold ground' became in my mind a significant irony that Mother Earth could be transformed into such a cold hard resting place for her own father.

When Laertes enters the scene, I clasped his face, echoing Roger in the nunnery scene, but in this case singing gently and weeping for the loss of everything good in her life – a direct contrast to Hamlet's spitting accusations. When I gave the rue to Claudius this became another moment of near explosion, as her guilt takes over the lucidity with which she sees the situation, generating 'And will a'not come again' (line 190) as a lament not only for her dead father but also as a direct apportion of the blame to herself. 'And we cast away moan' took on reverberations of the fact that we lose our feminine instincts because of political ambitions. Another gesture that occurred during one rehearsal was coincidentally an echo of the closet scene in which a distraught Gertrude clasps her son to her bosom and strokes his hair. Kenneth Branagh (Laertes) sank into my arms as Ophelia sings, whilst I stroked his hair, unaware at that point of the parallel mother / son image.

As these scenes began to take shape my instincts that she should appear strong and spirited in the first half of the play were reinforced. She provides in the mad scenes an alternative to the turn of events and an explanation that the 'humours' in the Prince are imbalanced. It is important therefore to see the balance in her own make-up, a vessel of enormous potential, destroyed by the forces of imbalance around her. Roger had pulled me downstage during the play scene to watch the action close to; it is irrefutable that she understands by this stage the consequences of his taking action against Claudius, but she is powerless to prevent it. She must offer an alternative only as an observer, catapulted along by the turn of

21 Ophelia with Laertes (Kenneth Branagh) in Act 4, Scene 5

events to her death. Then it becomes a tragedy. I came to understand why Ophelia is so often seen as weak: it is only in recent years that women have not become afraid of revealing the masculine qualities within them, something Shakespeare has always recognised. Visually I used a veil in the first mad scene in order to convey her feelings of guilt, wishing to hide her face for shame. It helped differentiate one scene from another, which is always an actress's problem with these scenes; I discarded the veil for her second entrance. By this time she feels she has something important to say, but because of her broken mind she is forced to use flowers to explain her thoughts. The flowers have obvious connotations, and because they are such beautiful delicate objects they associate themselves with Ophelia: if they are allowed to grow and bloom they will reappear the following season, strong and healthy; if they are picked too soon, they fade and die. In rehearsals I shamefully admitted my utter lack of knowledge of plant life by mistakenly handing rue to Laertes, fennel to the king, and daisies to the queen. A quick horticultural lesson later, and with the aid of labels on each flower provided by the stage manager, I managed to rectify this situation. 'Now *there's* a daisy' said Brian Blessed as Claudius.

By the time we arrived at the technical rehearsal stage, I felt justified in presenting my characterisation of Ophelia without having to resort to any histrionic displays of acting that are sometimes associated with the role. I received my reward just before we opened, when during a final run-through of the play in the rehearsal room, Sebastian Shaw, playing the First Grave-digger, a veteran of the RSC who first came to Stratford in 1926 to play Romeo, came over to me and said 'I have seen many Ophelias in my time, darling, but you are the first to have made me cry.' 'Because you think she's weak?', I asked. 'No', he replied, 'because you just wish Hamlet had told her of his worries. She would have known what to do.' Sebastian didn't realise what his remarks meant to me.

As the technical rehearsal progressed I was beginning to become more agitated. There comes a point when any extra rehearsals become counter-productive until you are firmly ensconced into the RST stage and begin to find the space, rather than be over-awed by it. I couldn't stop thinking about all the great actresses who had played on that stage, and each day filled me with more doubt about my own abilities at tackling my first ever Shakespeare. Whilst we were 'teching' the awkward grave sequence, in which I was to be lowered into a hole in the stage, wait to be picked up in the arms of Laertes, then dropped as he and Hamlet struggle over my body, one of the two trustworthy and strong stagehands who were to catch me as I fell, casually chatted to me as the tech. continued. I was to be buried in the black mourning dress I had worn for the mad scenes (not a nightgown in sight). My nerves about the opening night were at this point verging on the hysterical – I suppose as I wasn't playing Ophelia hysterically it had to come out in me. As we chatted away in this hole underneath the stage, the stagehand, who had been at the Memorial Theatre since its opening, said, 'I've caught them all down here you know, all the Ophelias.' 'Oh really', I replied, implying, I hoped, that this was not a good time to remind me of all the illustrious actresses who had played the role before. 'Oh yes', he said, 'Glenda Jackson, Helen Mirren, Carole Royle, yes I've caught them all you know. And they've all gone on to big things you know.' 'Yes', I replied weakly, I did know. 'Mind you', he answered, 'none of them was wearing as many clothes as you are.' Well, if only in the grave scene, I thought, at least I've made the character my own.

On reflection I think I only did succeed in making Ophelia my own as the run continued. The key to verse speaking, I discovered, is to go through all the processes Cis introduced me to and then once on stage forget all about them, use all the work put in during rehearsals to bring your character to life in front of an audience, and not worry about how many breaths you have just taken to complete a line. The luxury of the length of time you have at the RSC with the same role allowed me to put into practice all these new discoveries, until I truly felt in tune with this most difficult but fascinating of women. I was described by one critic as transforming from a 'purposeful Sloane Ranger, into a helpless urchin'; the first part of that description I surely had to hand to Cis.

The Fool in
King Lear

ANTONY SHER

ANTONY SHER played the Fool in Adrian Noble's production of *King Lear* at Stratford in 1982 and in London the following year. This, his first season with the RSC, of which he is an Associate Artist, also included the title role in Bulgakov's *Molière* and, in London in 1983, Tartuffe in Molière's play. Earlier work had included Buckingham in *Richard III* and another version of the Fool in *King Lear*. In 1984 he was back at Stratford to play Richard III. His book *Year of the King* describes his work on the part, which was seen in 1985 in London and the following year in Australia. Flote in Peter Barnes's *Red Noses* (for the RSC) and Arnold in *Torch Song Trilogy* were followed by his return to Stratford in 1987 to play Shylock, Malvolio, and Vindice in *The Revenger's Tragedy*. His films include *Superman II*, *Mark Gertler*, and *Shadey* and several television roles include that of Howard Kirk in *The History Man*.

Lear's Fool keeps cropping up in my life. In 1968 when I emigrated from South Africa to England, one of the first things I did was make a pilgrimage to Stratford-upon-Avon to see a performance by the Royal Shakespeare Company; as it happened it was Trevor Nunn's production of *King Lear* starring Eric Porter. It was to be my first encounter with both the RSC and what is arguably the greatest work by their resident dramatist. The matinee on that wet, August Saturday made an enormous impact on me, on many different levels, but most indelibly in my discovery of this character called the Fool. In that production he was beautifully played by Michael Williams with a grin permanently frozen on his face as if the clown had wiped off his cartoon make-up only to find that the crude outlines had stuck. I was haunted by both the actor's skill and the author's sense of the absurd and tragi-comic – qualities which I had previously thought were the inventions of twentieth-century dramatists like Becket and Ionesco. The Fool remained with me: four years later, with drama school and a brief spell in summer rep behind me, my first serious engagement as a professional actor

22   Antony Sher as the Fool, 1982

was playing the role at the Liverpool Everyman, and exactly ten years after that I was finally to join the RSC playing the role again.

In his introductory talk at the read-through for this latter production the director, Adrian Noble, mentioned two important elements in the play – the cruelty and the sense of the absurd. In the latter case he pointed to two examples – the Fool's soliloquy during the storm, with its curious anachronism ('This prophecy Merlin shall make, for I live before his time' (3.2.95–6)), and Gloucester hurling himself off an imaginary cliff. Adrian also stressed that we were in the privileged position of having almost three months to rehearse (because we were working alongside rehearsals for Edward Bond's play *Lear*) and therefore could afford to allow the production concept to grow indigenously from rehearsals rather than impose one, as is more frequently the case. He and the designer, Bob Crowley, had only vague ideas about the set and none about the costumes yet. This allowed the actors an enormous amount of creative freedom and space which was particularly valuable to me since the subsequent read-through, done very simply without any attempt at characterisation, served to remind me what I had already discovered ten years earlier in Liverpool – my own voice and personality didn't do the role any favours at all. In both productions I encountered the same two basic problems – what *character* to give the Fool, and how to make him *funny*.

Shakespeare doesn't give us any clues as to his *character* – his background, his appearance, his age. The King calls him 'Boy' but since he himself is 'fourscore and upwards' this is precious little help. The only reliable fact we are given about the character is his profession – he is a court jester. That leads to the second problem, how to make him believable as a comic performer – in other words *funny*. It seems to me always important that an audience should be able to believe the actor is capable of doing the job of work which his character has chosen as a profession, even if the action of the play is purely domestic and the actor is not required to do so on stage. Unfortunately in the case of the Fool, the actor *is* – his first scene (Act 1, Scene 4) requires him to perform for Lear and his knights.

The problem is compounded for me by the fact that I've always found Shakespeare's clowns the least funny characters imaginable. To some extent this is because a lot of their humour has not aged well, the jokes and puns have become very obscure (as in, for example, the Fool's lines '. . . thou shalt have as many dolours for thy daughters as thou canst tell in a year' (2.4.54)) and is not easily accessible to a modern audience. However, it is also the clown's *function* which has become outdated. Modern audiences find humour in the most unlikely places; they want humour to surprise them. Therefore in, say, *Twelfth Night*, Feste, the clown who comes on stage to-make-us-laugh, encounters a natural resistance, a slight chill, while the steward, Malvolio, encased in his own solemnity and self-importance, instantly touches our twentieth-century sense of humour – he is Basil in *Fawlty Towers* – and we laugh at his anger, his tumbling dignity, his pain. Our current sense of humour is in no way cute or coy.

Lear's Fool is obviously different from the Festes, Touchstones, Lancelot Gobbos, in that he is functioning within a tragedy, but the basic problem remains – he is supposed to be a professional comic. In Alan Dosser's 1972 Liverpool Everyman production, the solution was to create a character who was unintentionally funny – a rather nervous, twitchy little man in a huge coat, with a shaved head, and a lower jaw thrust forward in an underbite which caused the voice to sound slightly retarded and his wisdom to be trapped in goonish noises (the recurring word 'nuncle' sounded particularly apt in this voice). By using a speech impediment which appealed to the cruel humour of our (mainly young) audience, we had a character who was being laughed *at*, and who could then exploit that situation and reverse it. It had worked successfully, but I had no desire to import this fully formed characterisation into Adrian's new production. Anyway, the role is so inextricably linked to Lear himself, as a master–servant relationship, a double-act, that the two performances have to grow together in rehearsals, both actors and the director making their discoveries simultaneously. Adrian's own starting point for the Fool was the image of the strange banjo player in the film *Deliverance*: the baldish figure with pale eyes, looking both like a young boy and an old man, and seeming to have an eerie prescience of the horrific events to come.

Rehearsals proceeded on two levels for me: there were the conventional rehearsals with the rest of the cast, gradually exploring the text and the events of the play, with me having to busk through the role as neutrally as possible, but usually emerging uncomfortably as a nimble-footed cheeky chappie (a tradition of playing Shakespeare's fools which I dislike intensely); and then there were private experimental sessions with Adrian, Bob Crowley, and Michael Gambon (playing Lear) to try and find the *character* of the Fool and the relationship with his master.

The first breakthrough came in a rehearsal of the heath scenes when Adrian asked each of the actors involved to find an animal to play, in order to release the savagery and wildness of the situation. I chose a chimpanzee, chattering and clapping hands, hurling myself around in forward rolls, and found this very liberating for the role. That weekend I hurried to London Zoo to watch the chimps and became even more convinced that they had all the requisite qualities for the Fool – manic comic energy when in action, a disturbing sadness when in repose. A delightful coincidence that day at the zoo was rounding a corner to discover that Michael Gambon was also there, presumably also in search of his character, leaning against the plate-glass of the gorillas' cage, man and beast locked in solemn contemplation of one another.

One of the confusing aspects of building a character is when one uncovers what seems to be a brilliant solution only to find that its use isn't immediately apparent. The Fool isn't an animal, a chimp; it didn't help me in illuminating the speeches or in creating some kind of background for him. At the time it seemed that I had to abandon this route, but it does all go into the melting pot and when the final character eventually emerged I

23 Lear (Michael Gambon) and the Fool

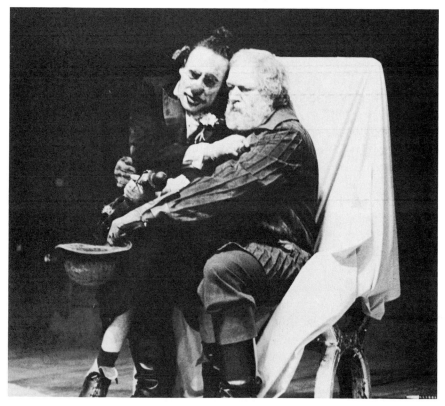

was delighted to discover that he had many simian qualities – he would run with long floppy arms held high, leap into people's arms, or hang from the ladders on the proscenium arch.

It also fascinates me how one's creative process is fed as much by chance as by careful deliberation. In that season at Stratford there was a production of *Macbeth* and the programme happened to contain a chronology of the Middle Ages with this entry for 1549: 'Court jesters (dwarfs, cripples) appear in Europe.' This seemed to be an interesting extension of what we had done vocally in Liverpool – a character exploiting his disability in order to survive, turning society's mockery of him to his advantage. The idea of a crippled clown immediately appealed to Adrian as well, enhancing the cruelty which he perceived in the play. This time a door had opened only to reveal a confusing option of corridors. What kind of disability should he have? Every crippled walk I tried seemed either to stem from the rickets of David Threlfall in *Nicholas Nickleby* or the spasticity of David Schofield in *The Elephant Man*, both brilliant recent performances of the disabled. Bob Crowley and I discussed other alternatives – playing the Fool in a wheelchair or pram, or else finding a way of me actually playing him as a dwarf. This piece of fancy had been inspired by an illustration in William Willeford's book *The Fool and his Sceptre* where the mediaeval concept of Man achieving wholeness was depicted literally – a figure with a circle for a body. At an experimental session I tied an actress's rehearsal skirt round my neck and squatted down inside it so that my body became an indistinct bundle with head, arms, and little feet sticking out. The only way of moving was to motor along on my arms or do chimp-like forward rolls. This quickly proved too painful and impractical to sustain. However, once again an abandoned concept produced an interesting residue – while experimenting in this way we had hit upon the somewhat surrealist idea of the dwarf growing to normal size during the Merlin speech (3.1.81–94) as he imagines a bizarre future time ('Then shall the realm of Albion / Come to great confusion') where there will be such chaos 'that going shall be us'd with feet'. Although not played as a dwarf in the eventual production, my crippled Fool did develop whole, normal limbs at this point and danced.

About half way through rehearsals, with me floundering around as I have indicated, Adrian proposed a different kind of experimentation for the Fool, forgetting about the *man* for the moment and concentrating instead on his *job* – finding out what kind of entertainer he should be. Adrian suggested investigating this by employing a system of different devices on successive days – a red nose, a mask, a mime-artist's white face,

24   Lear's Fool (the dwarf/bundle notion):
sketch by Antony Sher

and so on. We began with the red nose and in the event never went any further, it was so immediately successful. There is something very liberating about wearing a red nose, both externally and internally; you look, feel, and sound odd, exaggerated, caricatured. In a way, the red nose is the smallest version of the face mask, a device which is famous for its powers of releasing inhibition; at drama school I remember the mask class producing the most extraordinary breakthroughs of emotion and inventiveness in all of the students.

Now things began to fall into place very quickly. The red nose led naturally to associated accoutrements like a bowler hat, long shoes, a tailcoat. And now by retrieving a crippled walk, with feet and knees turned inwards, as well as a trace of the Liverpool Everyman lower-jaw underbite, the mixture was complete – the accoutrements of a clown worn clumsily but defiantly by a little crippled outcast – and both the *man* and his *job* were evident.

I have dwelt this long on the external image of the performance because it seems to me that there is a group of Shakespearean roles where it is as desirable for the actor to present a striking physical image as it is for him to do justice to the text and emotions; some other roles that are in this group that come to mind are Caliban, Ariel, Puck, Thersites, and Richard III.

As I have indicated, the journey towards finding this character was always made alongside the developing relationship between Lear and his Fool. The crucial thing is that it is *his* Fool, in the same way that someone who keeps a pet dog would have strong feelings about what breed, type, shape, and size they fancy. Luckily, Michael Gambon and I had discovered an immediate rapport as actors and friends and were able to feed this into the onstage relationship. Gambon's Lear was a king who enjoyed playing the fool himself and so many of the routines became double-acts – in their first big scene they played at being a ventriloquist and dummy, in their next scene they performed a music-hall front-cloth routine. This short scene (Act 1, Scene 5) while they are waiting for the horses to take them to Regan's castle, became central to my whole perception of their relation-

25   Lear's Fool: sketch by Antony Sher

ship. Adrian described it as a scene entirely to do with comic rhythm – a pattern of feed-and-punch-lines, a smokescreen of mindless humour – which Lear can then break by his sudden statements of heart-felt panic ('I did her wrong' or 'I will forget my nature'). By performing the jokes out-front, to an imaginary audience, like a game that friends might play, it made the beginning of Lear's breakdown very vivid and created a terrible panic in the Fool – he has never seen his master like this before. It was a brilliant notion of Adrian's, enhanced by the use of footlights and giant shadows, the two characters and their relationship literally illuminated in a bold piece of expressionist theatre.

There was a strong element of bravery, almost reckless bravery in the whole rehearsal process. It was Adrian's first main house production and he had an enormous appetite for the opportunities it presented for us all; he led us into areas where a more experienced and jaded foot might have refrained from treading. Rehearsals were always exhilarating and utterly unpredictable not only in their content but sometimes in their location.

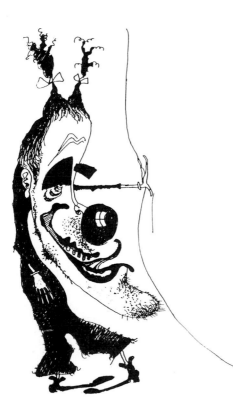

26   Lear's Fool: sketch by Antony Sher

One windy evening Adrian, Gambon, and I went up Dover's Hill, a local beauty spot, to work on the storm scenes. It was the spring of 1982 and the Falklands War was raging. Harrier jets from the nearby airbase would shoot by and Gambon used their terrifying, deafening noise to pit 'Blow winds' against.

Whenever we worked on the storm scenes back at the theatre, the composer, Ilona Sekacz, would be present, making the rehearsal room piano disgorge its most unmusical sounds. Adrian was insistent that the storm should be considered as another character in those scenes rather than as a sound effect to be just arbitrarily introduced at the technical rehearsal.

Ilona was also occupied in the equally ear-splitting task of teaching me how to play the tiny Suzuki violin which she and Adrian wanted the Fool to have. As a singer I am chronically tone deaf and my musical skills are subsequently non-existent. We therefore quickly decided that the Fool's playing of his violin should be somewhat individualistic, and further covered up my musical incompetence by finding other uses to which the violin, its bow and case could be put other than those for which they had been intended – for example, the instrument was strummed as a ukelele, the bow had many uses as a cane and prodder, and the case served as a useful phallic object to help the audience understand, 'She that's a maid now, and laughs at my departure / Shall not be a maid long, unless things be cut shorter' at the end of Act 1, Scene 5.

27   Lear's Fool: sketches by Antony Sher

All of this helped to develop the comic style of this particular jester, described by Goneril at one point as 'all-licens'd' – he was the kind of comic it would be very dangerous to heckle; an improviser who could take any object or statement and explore it for its every use and meaning. He improvises his way entirely through his first big scene, using a mixture of spontaneous wit and old routines; for example, when the King suddenly describes him as 'a bitter Fool' he instantly recites a little rhyme on that theme ('the sweet and bitter Fool'). In rehearsals I was learning how to make his performing style as unpredictable as possible, a Lenny Bruce type of comic, often taking the most dangerous subjects as his joke-material ('thou mad'st thy daughters thy mothers') at the risk of overstepping the mark and suffering the consequences of being whipped savagely for the

28   Lear's Fool: sketch by Antony Sher

amusement of the Knights, which was always Lear's method of getting the last laugh. Adrian was very strict about maintaining this element of improvisation, rather than the routines being pre-planned. In another of our outdoor rehearsals – this time in someone's garden – I came across some eggshells in a compost heap and held them over my eyes for the Fool's most savage indictment of Lear: 'Nuncle, give me an egg, and I'll give thee two crowns . . . When thou clovest thy crown i'th'middle and gav'st away both parts, thou bor'st thine ass on thy back o'er the dirt. Thou hadst little wit in thy bald crown when thou gav'st thy golden one away' (1.4.155–63). Although Adrian was taken with the dual image of blindness and prophecy, he wasn't content to let me use an egg in the production until I could come up with the explanation that the Fool had stolen one for his tea, happened to have it in his pocket at the time of being summoned to Lear, and so was improvising with it on the spur of the moment.

If the Fool is correctly established in his crucial opening scenes, while he is still functioning in his professional capacity, the rest of the part is relatively easy to play – a servant or pet loyally following his master into the abyss, increasingly incapable of helping or soothing Lear and eventually replaced by Poor Tom whose elemental violence acts like a drug in releasing the full force of Lear's madness, a more powerful 'hit' than the relatively safe anarchy which the Fool can provide.

For centuries scholars have puzzled over the sudden and inexplicable disappearance of the Fool from the play. He accompanies Lear, Kent, and Poor Tom throughout the storm scenes on the heath and then into the hovel where they enact a mock trial of Lear's daughters. During these scenes the character speaks less and less and with decreasing effectiveness indicating that he is probably becoming physically exhausted (by making him crippled we emphasised this) and that his function – both as a dramatic device and as a companion to Lear – is coming to an end. However, instead of exploiting the conclusion of this marvellous character, Shakespeare suddenly has him disappear after the hovel scene (Act 3, Scene 6) without any explanation or reference. One popular theory is that in the original production the same actor would have been playing both the Fool and Cordelia and was required to prepare for the latter role after the hovel scene; when Cordelia is dead Lear does describe her as 'my poor fool'. In effect the theory is suggesting that the author, who after all was churning out these plays fairly quickly, simply didn't have the time or inventive energy to write an 'exit' for the Fool. So what may just have been a careless oversight in the original production has been handed down to us as a frustrating enigma. Both Adrian and I were determined to try and offer the audience some kind of explanation for the disappearance and we discussed ways in which the Fool might remain behind in the hovel, exhausted and despairing, despite Kent's last reference to him: 'Come, help to bear thy master; / Thou must not stay behind' (3.6.100–1).

Then one day a different solution presented itself. Adrian had asked stage management to create the environment of a hovel using bits of debris (an oil drum, boxes, and sacks); we then busked freely through the scene seeking to release the lunacy, panic, and desperation all the characters are experiencing by this stage. The rehearsal was wild and dangerous, feathers from a ripped pillow filling the air. Gambon delivered his line, 'Then let them anatomize Regan; see what breeds about her heart' (3.6.76–7), as a direct instruction to me. I grabbed a pillow, jumped in the oil drum and proceeded to 'anatomize' it savagely. The next time we ran through the scene I happened to be already holding the pillow when that line occurred, so this time Gambon attacked it himself with his knife, hacking and stabbing. Afterwards we cautiously discussed the possibility of Lear stabbing through the pillow and thus accidentally killing the Fool. As the idea grew it became apparent that it could be incorporated into the rest of the scene without any great strain: soon after that moment the Fool has to speak his enigmatic last line – 'And I'll go to bed at noon' (line 85) – which would make perfect sense coming from a mortally wounded man, and the other characters simply failed to notice what has happened to him, their concentration being fixed entirely on Lear's collapse. Then they all exit from the scene calling back to the Fool who attempts to clamber out of the oil drum and follow, but instead collapses back dead. We had accidentally stumbled upon a valid and, I believe, uncontrived explanation for the Fool's disappearance – he was a chance casualty of the crazy night on the heath. A very different solution to the same problem, but one which I also like, was used in the famous Russian film of the play, where the Fool *doesn't* disappear, but becomes mute after the storm and remains with Lear throughout the rest of the story, a silent witness to the tragedy he has prophesied.

A production often reflects the nature of its rehearsal period, whether it has been happy or fraught or, as in this case, full of bold and thrilling invention. The feeling among the whole Company when we first opened in Stratford was that we clearly had an exciting and dangerous interpretation of the play to offer and the response of the audience (and even the critics!) was thrilling. Part of the joy of working in the theatre is being present when

29   Lear's Fool: painting by Antony Sher

these rare currents are flowing; part of the frustration is trying to recreate that kind of buzz over a long run. In this case, by the time of the London opening a year later, we seemed to have lost some of our initial boldness. For example, there had been a loss of faith in the 'front cloth' scene and it became a pale imitation of what it had been in Stratford. Similarly, I was unable to make the Fool's routines work as effectively as before and was incapable of making the audience actually laugh out loud – my original goal – which had been effortlessly achieved the previous year in Stratford. I think the originality of the production was consequently reduced because I believe that tragedy is often heightened by the close proximity of comedy. Although the London run was personally upsetting at the time, now in retrospect it doesn't seem worth dwelling on – the theatre is so full of magic it should not really surprise us when some of it vanishes into thin air.

For me the Fool remains one of the most intriguing characters Shakespeare wrote, elusive and difficult to read on the printed page, but often very effective in performance. In some ways you could describe the writing as half-finished, a sketch; for the actor this is challenging and also flattering because Shakespeare is allowing us to fill in the missing spaces. However, as often happens in the theatre, we tend to focus too obsessively on our own role; in the end it is Lear's play, Lear's story, and seen in that context the Fool's disappearance is not difficult to explain at all – he has simply been absorbed by Lear, replaced by his madness, digested as fodder for his new perception of the world. For me one of the most moving moments in the play is when the mad Lear meets the blind Gloucester and comments to him, 'When we are born, we cry that we are come / To this great stage of fools.' Lear's journey through the play is a terrible and traumatic one, but before he dies he has learned compassion, humility, gentleness. Although no longer present to witness this transformation, the Fool would definitely have approved; of that I am sure.

Othello

BEN KINGSLEY

BEN KINGSLEY played Othello in Terry Hands's production at Stratford in 1985 and thereafter at the Barbican. He is an Associate Artist of the RSC and his work for the Company, which he first joined in 1967, includes (among much else) Demetrius in Peter Brook's production of *A Midsummer Night's Dream*, Ariel in *The Tempest* (for which he also wrote the music), Hamlet in Buzz Goodbody's Other Place production, Ford in *The Merry Wives of Windsor*, Brutus in *Julius Caesar*, and Squeers in *Nicholas Nickleby*. For the National Theatre he has appeared in *Volpone*, *The Country Wife*, and *The Cherry Orchard*. His one-man show *Kean* brought him to Othello by way of one of the role's most famous performers. His many film and television appearances include the leading roles in *Gandhi*, *Betrayal*, and *Silas Marner*.

Let me say at the outset that, whilst attempting a 'passionate indifference', I am addicted (amongst other things) to a harmony too rarely glimpsed. There are days that shimmer on the landscape of our lives, as a mirage – or a milestone. I had been in Marakesh for two weeks, filming *Harem*, directed by Arthur Joffe, with Nastassja Kinski as my co-star. Typically, on my days off, I enjoyed further exploring not only Marakesh but the internal landscape of the Prince I was portraying. An Arab. So on the evening of Sunday the 16th I was seated on my red stone balcony dressed in a black kaftan and sandals, gazing over the gardens of the Mamounia hotel. My eyes swept over the lawns, olive groves, lemon, orange and palm trees, the frangipani, the bougainvillea, and rested on the snow-capped Atlas mountains. The sun was setting on North Africa and the Mediterranean, a shower of shimmering orange and violet light provoking in me the simplest of questions 'how have I lived without this landscape till now?' Sharing my balcony was one of the artistes from our film. She not only acted in our film, but had also to be filmed drawing a portrait of my character. So there she sat, her African braided hair falling over her easel as she quietly worked

30   Ben Kingsley as Othello: painting by Dominique Benjamen

away at various studies of me, 'the Prince'. In that hour, as the sky turned deepest angry red, then black, amidst the absurdity and beauty that conspired almost to halt time itself, the telephone in my hotel room rang with a jarring insistency threatening to break the moment. But the moment held. My caller was Terry Hands, joint artistic director of the RSC. The role he invited me to consider was Othello. My reaction was immediate and (given the extraordinary circumstances) positive. 'Oh', said a surprised Terry, 'I thought you would need a long time to consider.' 'Why', I retorted, 'don't you think it's a good idea?' Thus, with a laugh, we concluded our conversation. I returned to my chair on the balcony; my life, and the portrait my colleague was attempting, had both changed. The seed had been implanted. The process of gestation had begun. My peripheral vision began to filter into my subconscious eye information that would sustain the rehearsal process and nourish the performance. A silhouette immediately began to uncoil itself, as if something dormant were being roused. As I said, at the time I was portraying an Arab – a twentieth-century Arab with a fourteenth-century soul. I was predisposed to the temperament and pace around me: the fraternally sensual embraces of the men; the young women emerging from purdah, vulnerable, beautiful, and still startled; the sipping of mint tea; and immensely polite and gently murmured conversations with bedouins over the exquisite quality of a carpet or the place of God in the universe (the stillness of them, the potential violence of them, fascinated me). My daily visits to the Hamman, the Turkish bath where through the swirling steam and almost annihilating heat, the face and body of Othello would emerge seated on the marble opposite me.

The spell that hovered over Marakesh remained unbroken. Peter Brook is one of my voices. By that I mean that I treasure his responses to any project of mine. We need such guides, such mentors and friends. His voice hailed me across the swimming pool of the Mamounia hotel. He was there! I poured out my latest news. We spent many hours together over the next few days. It was good to hear his voice. My wife, too, joined me in Marakesh for a few days, bringing a copy of *Othello* with her; so I began to read the play very slowly. A few days later Fabia Drake and I met for the first time; she too was staying at the Mamounia. From our first meeting, she too became a treasured voice. Her response to my playing Othello was immediate, vigorous, and caring. Here is an extract from one of the many letters that passed between her hotel room and mine. 'I have thought much about the wonderful task that lies ahead of you. Probably the most challenging of them all – and we haven't had one this century. . . I have a precious copy of George Henry Lewes at home who writes most vividly about the Italian actor Salvini as Othello, dilating upon his "afterswell of emotion" which I have never found mentioned before – I would lend it to you but you only need the play. It's Ben's Othello that lies ahead. No one else's. Yours ever, Fabia Drake. P.S. Moor or Blackamoor? If the former you might find his physical counterpart here. There are many whose visages carry the "shadowed livery of the burnished sun" and there is extreme elegance in some of those cloaked figures who frequent our lounges. F.'

One Sunday, Fabia and I drove out to lunch through torrential rain, with Adil, my proud and handsome driver at the wheel. Sitting with her in the back of the car I felt in the presence of a force which denied all that is said to be ephemeral about our craft. Her passion for Shakespeare and her knowledge of all those who have interpreted his works transcends time. She spoke again of Othello, recalling what George Henry Lewes had said about Salvini and Kean. Her words were an infusion. They would reverberate again and again in rehearsals and in performance. All too soon it was time for her to leave Morocco, and in turn, I too bade farewell to what had become my 'antres vast and deserts idle, rough quarries, rocks and hills whose heads touch heaven'. Farewell to Casablanca, Ouarzazate and the Atlas Mountains, and home to Stratford-upon-Avon.

I take pains with my preface, because I wish to stress how much courage I had to find to walk into the rehearsal room – courage, or ammunition. The first day of rehearsal is the means whereby we arrive at the second day's rehearsal, and then the work begins. Work on the text was educative and illuminating, and under Terry's brilliant and loving guidance, we were very soon to discover the great inner stress each character brought onto the stage, and that such a collection of sensibilities and temperaments locked together on a small island would inevitably lead to bloody catastrophe. Each tragic case history revealed itself in the writing to be a classic and immaculate syndrome that would bear scrutiny from the most searching of analysts. We were rehearsing a dangerous play, where safe routes and hiding places were useless. Even the rehearsal room was bare, as the beautiful set designed by Ralph Koltai was to be. 'Give me a place to stand' I said to Terry arrogantly in the early stages of rehearsal, quoting Archimedes, 'and I'll move the world.' He and Ralph gave us a gladiatorial arena, where our 'place to stand', where our every movement and word, were to be dictated by the degree and nature of passion experienced and expressed. Thus Terry locked the actors onto each other, not onto the furniture. He provided a context in which we could grapple only with our passions and with each other, and through which our only expression and release was the text. David Suchet (Iago) and I were to discover in exploring two faces of the same disturbed spirit, that this approach was exhilarating and profoundly exhausting. Rehearsal for me is the meticulous making of a mould, the creation through the text and one's body of a silhouette into which, in performance, one pours the white hot molten metal of the character. Everything must go into the crucible, as base metal. Here Terry's affection and provocation were vital. All my vulnerabilities, my history, my information and experience, my childhood and my manhood and more had to be hurled into that crucible in the quest for the gold that is Othello. We all bring our own limits to a piece of work, and hope that to a certain degree these frontiers will grow. We bring private knowledge to a public role, and without the trust of one's colleagues, this, to the vulnerable actor, can be a great risk. I understand the state of exile. I understand a need to belong. This was Kean's fatal disease. I comprehend this not through experience so much as observation. My father was born in East Africa – the son of Gujerat parents. He spent his childhood in an Islamic community born of the ancient Arab trade routes. My father came to England in 1927 at the age of fourteen and valiantly matured at an English public school, university, Guy's Hospital and then as a general practitioner in the north of England. He returned neither to East Africa nor Gujerat (India); to the landscapes that had nourished his pride, his myths, and his morality, to the home of his revered father, a king amongst men. I think this bred in him a sense of displacement. His beautiful English bride, a fashion model and actress, was his perfect Desdemona, and I hasten to add no one conspired to destroy them. But I know the chaos that could rise up in his throat when our English landscape became too alien. I could see the cry behind his eyes when our world baffled his ancient soul. 'I want to go home' they used to say; and 'I want to go home' went into the crucible to be coined night after night during Othello's disintegration.

Terry encouraged great stillness in me to counterweight the disintegration. Stillness was a vital ingredient for my crucible. Here I drew upon those resources that were developed whilst working on Gandhi with Richard Attenborough in India. I learned then to keep chaos at bay. I was Attenborough's chosen hero in India amongst millions of Indians, portraying the father of their nation. Fear and chaos could so easily have overwhelmed me, but with guidance from my colleagues I was able, like a general, to bear the enormous responsibility Richard had placed on my shoulders, and to share the power of those days that we seemed masters of. It was my first truly epic role, and Richard taught me to keep the integrity of each moment intact, and at the same time remain aware of the sweep of the whole event – a great lesson when applied to Othello. I left India as an Actor; I felt I had at last earned that role in life. Miraculously my next role was Raymond FitzSimons's Edmund Kean, directed by my wife Alison Sutcliffe. Unseen forces had brought Kean and me together within a week of my leaving India. It was during my work on Edmund Kean that the seeds of the possibility of playing Othello were sown, and the desire to play Othello germinated. FitzSimons chose as the central theme of his superb monologue the great soliloquy 'Oh now forever farewell the tranquil mind – farewell content', first to mark the emergence in the provinces of what was to become the jewel of his repertoire, then to underline the parallel tragedy of Kean's personal life, betrayed as he was by his mistress Charlotte Cox and publicly humiliated as a result, and finally to illustrate his death. Kean collapsed on the Covent Garden stage uttering the lines 'Othello's occupation's gone', fell into the arms of Charles his son, his Iago, and died a few days later, an expended meteor, victim of his own passions, breaker of his own limits. Kean suffered the pain of the outsider, the exile, lying his way into mocking and incredulous society by claiming to be the bastard son of the Duke of Norfolk. 'I fetch my life and being from men of royal siege' could have been Kean's primal cry, only, of course, to have his Irish gypsy background constantly alluded to. 'A triumph of genius against prejudice' is how Frances Wemyss describes Kean's career – a triumph, but at such a cost. A temperament addicted to a harmony that only applause, stardom, and victory on a colossal scale can begin to provide; a temperament that cannot, dare not, must not ever lose face. 'My *name*, that was as fresh / As Dian's visage, is now begrim'd and black / As mine own face' – 'My *name!*'

So into the crucible goes the unique destiny of an actor I have neither seen nor heard, but know and love as few can know and love Edmund Kean.

My capacity for great and violent jealousy has never been put to the test. Here my imagination had to act as catalyst. I know those who suffer the pangs of great jealousy, and that jealousy is consistent with an inner dread, and that inner dread is consistent in turn with their greatness. Their very stature in the world is based upon a desperate attempt to hold certain aspects of life as far away from them as possible. The distance between the ever potential chaos and the carefully modulated harmony is measured in their power, ability, strength, political accuracy, wealth, and status. I have tried to be more vulnerable to life, allowing life to happen to me as much as that is possible; I have no desire to make history. I know my craft is ephemeral. My strength, if I have any, lies in my vulnerability, not in my insistence on being invulnerable. 'No, not much moved' is Othello's first line of defence. Of course there are many inconsistencies between myself and Othello; therein lies the leap. It is fruitless to insist on playing aspects of oneself. I am a portrait artist; I am not the 'sitter', but the 'painter'. Often the greater the gap between an aspect of a character and its equivalent in me, the more exhilarating the leap. And without risk there is nothing beautiful or romantic in life. So into my crucible goes not *my* jealousy, but my 'content'; my 'tranquil mind', both at work and at home, and thus the measure of my pain were I to discover my 'occupation's gone'.

I had to seek out Othello's violence and bring it to the surface. Here, the leap was reduced to a mere hop. I see no contradiction in my need for harmony and peace and my capacity for great and sudden violence. If in life I am provoked beyond a certain level in certain areas I begin to taste violence in my mouth like an enzyme suddenly secreted and flushed through my system. I have learned to control it, to ritualize it, as have the Japanese, the most polite and most violent of peoples, and the Apaches. (It is very fortunate that I am an actor and not a criminal.)

Thus from the beginning of rehearsal a being emerged who, if provoked at a primal level, would react with the violence of a psychopath; a being in a 'molten' state, and an etched course for him to follow in performance.

In the etching, gouging, and scooping out of that course, Terry and I realized that while Iago plays the transitions, Othello expresses the changed states. Othello's emotional journey echoed Fabia's words in the car. I remember her telling me what George Henry Lewes had said about Salvini, who was thought to be a wonderful Othello; Lewes dwelt upon the 'afterswell of emotion' – an essential pivot in the technique of acting. Lewes's writing in his brilliant book on *Actors and the Art of Acting* in 1875 tells of the 'truth of passion, namely the expression of subsiding emotion'. He goes on:

Edmund Kean's instinct taught him what few actors are taught, that a strong emotion after discharging itself in one massive current continues for a time expressing itself in feebler currents. The waves are not stilled when the storm has passed away, there remains the groundswell troubling the depths. In watching Kean's quivering muscles and altered tones you felt the subsidence of passion. The voice might be calm but there was a tremor in it. The face might be quiet but there were vanishing traces of the recent agitation.

Thus George Henry Lewes. He thought that Kean was far better than Salvini in this showing of the subsiding emotion:

and it is impossible to over-estimate the verisimilitude that such a truth would give to a performance . . . Great grief does not subside when the sobs are quietened. Great joy does not evaporate when its cause has been absorbed. The afterglow of both states, if perfectly conceived by a player, continues and is like a refrain running through the mind irrespective of what is being said.

This is the level of commitment such a role demands; only refined gold can be one's metal. Rehearsals are a catalogue of mistakes punctuated by cries for help. The role of Othello is the highest of challenges and would be unplayable, even distressing and corrosive, if the actor in that role were unhappy about his appearance, the setting, and the colleagues around him. As for my appearance, Terry, Alex Reid, and I met before rehearsals began, to discuss this vital aspect. Moor, certainly; we were instantly agreed on that, and it would be absurd not to capitalize on my recent Arabian experience and not to use my own silhouette and features. When I saw the portrait (portraits – they are wonderful things, talismans, echoes and mirrors) of the Moor at the court of Queen Elizabeth I, owned by the Shakespeare Institute, I knew we had found a thrilling starting point, and Alex and Terry responded generously to what information I could give in those early exploratory days. Thus when I saw the drawings of Othello in his various garments, I felt already integrated with the hugely complex process of presenting a play on the Stratford stage. As for my wig, that was based on a fabulous head of hair I encountered in Morocco. Brenda Leedham and I worked together on the creation of it. Thus emerged the braids of black, red, gold, and white that fell down to my shoulders.

As rehearsals progressed so the appearance was refined in the fitting room. I found myself staring at a man in the mirror that I was still struggling to comprehend. By the end of the final run-through in the rehearsal room, we knew we were ready to place our play on the main stage and that the next great phase of work was upon us. I stepped out of my white Moroccan rehearsal robe, put my Samurai rehearsal sword to rest, and put on Othello's clothes, his dagger, his scimitar.

The arena into which we stepped was one of Ralph Koltai's finest achievements: a chamber of sculptured light composed of black and white perspex, and huge sheets of gauze framed in glowing fibre optics, capable of being both epic and domestic. One did not have to search for the predicament on every entrance, there it was, held by one's fellow actors and contained by columns, shafts, and sheets of black and white light. We had been given a place to stand. I had not been on stage for two years, but thanks to Cicely Berry's guidance through a minefield of mostly my own inadequacies, I was able to breathe, speak, and begin to play the building on the dress rehearsal and those early performances. She helped me place all my information into my breath, into my voice.

It is said that the shock experienced by an actor walking onto a stage is equivalent to that experienced in a minor motor accident. It can take many minutes for the actor to recover his true rhythm. Terry gave me an entrance that simply outlawed shock. There was no space for such a hiatus. It was the slowest, longest, calmest of entrances; centre stage and also in a follow-spot of light; dressed from head to foot in white, so the slightest falter would have registered. Contrary to the usual gulps for breath, shaky legs, and pounding heart experienced in the wings before an entrance, I was

31 'If after every tempest come such calms'
Desdemona (Niamh Cusack) and Othello arrive in Cyprus

steady, still, and calm. Othello was indestructible! What a preface to the later disintegration. In my secret play the man that he had always wanted to be enters the arena; the man he and I dread being leaves the arena by committing suicide. And the crucible of molten metal must be drained and *seen* to be drained every night.

Only those who have played Othello know how uniquely distressing the role can sometimes be. When the barriers dissolve, when pressures on the actor and the dilemma of the character fuse into a subjective pain in front of your audience then these are dark nights, and no amount of applause can set the actor free. The very soul seems metabolized. The play smoulders on in the body and brain until the early hours, and the only way to rid oneself of the burning restlessness is to do the play again. Yet is not this 'the afterswell of emotion' simply seeping through the chamber and into life. Imperative perhaps. It took all my physical and mental powers to maintain my passionate indifference, to confine the 'afterswell' to the theatre: on those nights, both the character and I were released; it was this struggle, this battle, that led to a growth on stage, a development of my technique. It had to, or I'd perish. My voice grew to contain and express the pain; my body gained strength from facing the gladiatorial arena night after night. For example, Shakespeare in his genius places the 'fit' in the first scene of Act 4. Here, in my secret play, is where Othello and I feel such a crushing inexpressible pain that we attempt to leave the arena. We wished to bleach out all definition in one massive electric discharge. Of course this catharsis was achieved technically night after night; I never injured myself but the fit left me stunned, and the emergence from it only to find Othello still in the play, still in great pain, and even more humiliated and vulnerable is a state I shall never forget. It was Iago/David that provoked Othello/me back into that monstrous play – to face the inevitable unfolding of Act 4 and Act 5. It was Desdemona who provoked the galvanizing violence of the slap that breaks the numbing voltage – the 'afterswell' of the fit. Thus it was an incandescent anger that had to be directed, paced, and ruthlessly motivated to fuel the journey through Acts 4 and 5 to stillness again in the final address and then suicide. The final honourable action left to Othello. It was this quest for both rage and lucidity that taught me to go beyond known limits, through a rawness and looseness born of exhaustion and exertion, night after night.

Why go through such barriers? Real actors never shrug their shoulders in the wings and ask such dead-end questions. Where else can I place the energy I was born with? The energy of the nomad, to whom distance is irrelevant and whose house is his soul. Yes, I am addicted to a harmony too seldom glimpsed, that can be experienced in the midst of great turmoil and passion. If this is my drug, I have no wish to withdraw. This all could read as a catalogue of my needs and perhaps my gifts are born of my flaws. It doesn't matter here. If everything were neatly dovetailed together where would be the leap, and for me the leap is all. In his essay 'On Drama' in *The Myth of Sisyphus* Albert Camus writes:

the actor's realm is that of the fleeting. Of all kinds of fame, it is known his is the most ephemeral . . . From the fact that everything is to die some day he draws the best conclusion. An actor succeeds or does not succeed. A writer has some hope even if he is not appreciated. He assumes that his works will bear witness to what he was. At best the actor will leave us a photograph, and nothing of what he was himself, his gestures and his silences, his gasping or his panting with love will come down to us, for him not to be known is not to act, and not acting is dying a hundred times with all the creatures he would have brought to life or resuscitated . . . He is a traveller in time and, for the best, the hunted traveller, pursued by souls.

Camus too, is one of my voices.

Now Othello has left my repertoire:

> If after every tempest come such calms,
> May the winds blow till they have waken'd death!
> And let the labouring bark climb hills of seas
> Olympus-high, and duck again as low
> As hell's from heaven!

There remains a sense of joy in achievement, and gratitude to Terry Hands, who, having eyes – chose me.

But there's more; during the last glorious week of the London run, when scores of spring flowers were thrown onto our stage during the curtain call, a large tubular package arrived for me at the stage door. I took it back to my London flat, but did not open it immediately. When I did I wept. It is a magnificent oil portrait of my Othello by Dominique Benjamen, 'a gift', she wrote, 'from one portrait artist to another'. So the wheel had turned full circle – from the portrait on the balcony below the Atlas mountains to the house on the edge of the Cotswolds, where the portrait of my Moor now hangs, and where I keep my letters from Fabia Drake.

Iago in
Othello

DAVID SUCHET

DAVID SUCHET played Iago in Terry Hands's production of *Othello* at Stratford in 1985 and in the following season at the Barbican. He first worked for the RSC, of which he is an Associate Artist, in 1973, when his parts included Tybalt, Orlando, and the King of Navarre. Among his numerous roles for the Company since then have been Caliban (on which he wrote for the first *Players of Shakespeare* collection), Grumio, Bolingbroke in *Richard II*, Edward IV in *Richard III*, and Shylock, as well as Herman Glogauer in *Once in a Lifetime*, first at the Aldwych and later in the West End. Other stage work includes his one-man show *The Kreutzer Sonata* and most recently *Separation*, and among numerous film and television appearances are the title roles in *Freud* and *Blott on the Landscape*.

The telephone rings. 'Hello, Terry here.' Pause. 'Terry Hands.' 'Oh, my God, *Terry* – hello, how are you?' 'Fine – look – I would like to do a production of *Othello* with Ben Kingsley in the title role and we (Ben and I) have talked and, well – would you consider playing Iago?'

It is unnecessary to relate the rest of the conversation (apart from not accurately remembering it) but necessary to note that it took place in December 1984 and that I finally said yes in April 1985. *Five* months to reach a decision to play one of the finest and most famously complex characters in Shakespeare? Why? Well, precisely because of one word – *fear*!

I had read the play, of course, seen it, knew it well, and decided to go to the Shakespeare Centre to read the reviews of the play since the RSC had first performed it. What surprised me (even apart from the relative unpopularity of the play in this century) was the scarcity of successful Iagos. How odd, I thought, especially since this character is so famous. It was at the Shakespeare Centre I learned that Iago had been played mainly as a smiling villain. Emrys James (RSC, 1971) had been very different – a

32   David Suchet as Iago, 1985

psychotic maniac of an NCO in the army – laughing almost maniacally as he looked on the result of his machinations, the bodies of Desdemona and Othello.

Reading about the play I learned of its performance history in the eighteenth and nineteenth centuries. Here the play was more successful, indeed perhaps the most popular of Shakespeare's plays. Here also were great performances of Iago and Othello. Edwin Booth as Iago and Kean as Othello stand out at different times. But what is important is that the *play* itself was accepted and popular. Why, I puzzled, did it not have the same effect on our twentieth-century audiences and critics?

I then read (seemingly mountainous!) essays of literary criticism about the play and centred my readings on Iago himself. This research covered just about everything from Coleridge's 'motiveless malignity' to essays about him being an emissary from the devil. All my reading made me aware that almost everyone that has either written about Iago or played Iago, is always in search of one thing: *motivation*. The search for motivation in any character is a necessary step to understanding the behaviour of that character. But no one has ever come up with a completely satisfying explanation for Iago's behaviour. Instead we get a series of labels:

1. A smiling villain.
2. The latent homosexual.
3. The devil's emissary.
4. The playwright (i.e. creator of events and observer, who conducts the outcome).
5. The melodramatic machiavel.

Putting these 'labels' on a characterisation is a convenient though simplistic way around the problem, allowing the actor to play the role effectively irrespective almost of his Othello. Hence the play becomes a battle about who is going to win the applause of the critics and of the audience. And hence the play does not work because the play itself can never really come to the surface – only two (or possibly one) bravura performances.

Our rehearsal period was approximately six weeks and we started with a detailed analysis of the play. My personal plan for rehearsal was to try out all the various labels which I have mentioned above. It was a most interesting experience because each way/label came unstuck at certain places in the play and I had to bend the text to make the 'label' work. Having concluded that I would not play just one of the labels I decided to find out not *how* to play Iago but *why* Shakespeare wrote him. What does he provide, why did Shakespeare need him?

To do this I read the play without Iago in it. Basically Othello marries Desdemona, her father is upset, but the Duke appeases him. Othello goes off to Cyprus with Desdemona. When they arrive the wars have ended and (without Iago's machinations) there is no reason why everyone couldn't have had a very nice holiday!

What is missing is what causes all the destruction in the play – Jealousy. Iago *represents* Jealousy, *is* Jealousy. What is Iago jealous about?

1. Not becoming a lieutenant (jealous over Cassio).
2. Jealous that Emilia and Othello have had an affair.
3. Jealous of Emilia and Cassio.
4. Jealous over Desdemona and Cassio.
5. Jealous of Desdemona's power over Othello.

But what struck me was that all these reasons that he states as justifications for his actions are totally unfounded.

1. When Othello makes Iago lieutenant ('Now art thou my lieutenant') Iago does not stop his destructive actions.
2. There is no evidence anywhere in the text, let alone in the scenes where Emilia and Othello are alone, that there has been any form of sexual liaison or indeed of any other kind between them.
3. Because of one line at the sea shore?
4. Because Desdemona is 'fram'd as fruitful / as the free elements' and Cassio has a 'daily beauty in his life which makes me ugly'?

There is no doubt that Iago is *genuinely* jealous of these things; therefore (I wondered) could Iago destroy and kill through jealousy even though the reasons for his jealousy are unfounded? Human beings are given to finding justifications for deeds or actions to make those deeds 'allowable' in their own minds even though they are not always valid justifications. And so it is with Iago.

Then comes another 'Why?', this time in reference to his jealousy. Why is he jealous? When Desdemona is wondering why Othello may be jealous (3.4.158), Emilia/Shakespeare gives us one answer to the problem:

> But jealous souls will not be answer'd so;
> They are not ever jealous for the cause,
> But jealous for they're jealous. It is a monster
> Begot upon itself, born on itself.   (3.4.159–62)

In other words, *don't look for reasons for the behaviour of jealous people.*

Critics, actors, and audiences will constantly ask 'why does Iago do this or that? why is he jealous?' Emilia, his wife, who knows him better than anyone, gives us the answer – Don't ask!

I also considered Iago's behaviour pattern through the play and his relationships with other characters. Perhaps the most important relationship up to Act 2, Scene 3, is with Roderigo. I noted that in the conversations that they have, Roderigo hardly ever says a word. In the first eighty-two lines of the play, Roderigo and Iago are alone on stage. Iago has seventy-two and a half lines, Roderigo nine and a half. In Act 1, Scene 3, beginning with Roderigo's 'Iago' down to Roderigo's exit, 'I'll sell all my land', Iago has seventy-eight lines, Roderigo fifteen lines. And in Act 2, Scene 1, Iago has sixty-eight lines and Roderigo six lines.

But during these scenes we see Iago at his most pained and most voluble. Shakespeare is using Roderigo as a foil to Iago in the form of aided soliloquy. Iago never charms Roderigo; in fact quite the opposite – he tells Roderigo some hateful things about life and indeed about the woman with whom Roderigo is infatuated.

It is now necessary to look at each scene as I did in the rehearsal room. What I tried to do was to approach every moment of the role without preconception or labels. In Act 1, Scene 1, we see Iago justifying his hatred of Othello to Roderigo because Othello has made Cassio his lieutenant and not Iago. But there seemed to me something else going on behind all this volubility over Cassio. The audience doesn't know, but Iago and Roderigo do know, that Othello has got married. For Iago Othello's marrying means that their friendship (Othello's and his) will never be the same again. It's only because of the wedding that Othello needs the unpractised 'bookish theoric' – the Sandhurst type – to be his lieutenant as a status symbol.

> Preferment goes by letter and affection,
> Not by the old gradation, where each second
> Stood heir to th' first. (1.1.36–8)

Also, I noted that it is quite possible from the text that Iago has been *promoted* to the officer class of Ancient (albeit the lowest officer rating), from the ranks:

> He (*in good time!*) must his lieutenant be,
> And I (God bless the mark!) his Moorship's ancient. (1.1.32–3)

If this is so, Iago's promotion is an even bigger snub if we accept that Othello knew of his desire to become lieutenant:

> Three great ones of the city,
> In personal suit to make me his lieutenant,
> Off-capp'd to him. (1.1.8–10)

There is *every* reason, in fact, to believe Othello *does* know because of his extraordinary 'Now art thou my lieutenant' (3.3.479) later on.

Iago therefore sees his whole life beginning to change and his close relationship to Othello is already fading. At the same time, the scene emphasises Iago's ambition. He wants to stop the wedding and in doing so tries to cause chaos. I found the imagery of Iago's speech,

> Do, with like timorous accent and dire yell
> As when, by night and negligence, the fire
> Is sped in populous cities (1.1.75–7)

rather extreme and grotesque. It is a war image coming from the mouth of a soldier, an image of death, but an image which obviously excites Iago.

Chaos achieved with the waking of Brabantio, he leaves to find Othello and when we next see Iago, he is speaking to Othello quite differently from the way he spoke with Roderigo. We also see a different character from the embittered, angry, hurt, resentful figure in the first scene; now we see a dog yapping around the heels of his master. The immaturity of Iago's dialogue is brilliantly counterpointed in Othello's haughty calmness.

It is true, in this scene, for the first time, we do see Iago being two-faced (he swears, aptly, 'by Janus', the two-faced god). And interestingly, after the entrance of Brabantio in Act 1, Scene 2, up to Othello's and Desdemona's exit in Act 1, Scene 3, Iago does not say a word. With a character as voluble as Iago, his silences are as important as his dialogue. It is Iago who goes off to get Desdemona and therefore is not allowed to hear Othello's florid, and beautiful, tale of his wooing Desdemona. How ironic that when he finishes it is Iago who brings her in and delivers her silently to Othello and the Duke. This section is filled (for Iago) with the hope that the Duke will intercede and divorce them (i.e. chaos again) and very intensive listening. But the Duke is satisfied that Desdemona and Othello have married out of love and he consents that she go to the wars in Cyprus with Othello. For Iago, his relationship with Othello will not be the same again – a woman, Othello's wife, will be the Moor's companion and confidante. What is more, Othello asks Iago to bring his wife, Emilia, to look after Desdemona.

Iago's world is now changing very fast indeed. He is surrounded by happy people: soldiers pleased to go to war; Othello happy in marriage and the prospect of his taking his young bride to the wars; Cassio happy that in so short a time he will be taking part in an active campaign. Three people, however, are not so happy. Brabantio has lost his daughter and warns Othello, 'She has deceived her father, and may thee' and Roderigo, besotted with Desdemona, is now in utter despair. And of course, Iago's plans have failed. Confronted by Roderigo who announces he is going to 'incontinently drown myself' it is as if a trigger has been pulled in Iago's head and he sprays the stage, Roderigo, and the audience with some very downright and earthy attitudes to life and living. He starts as a confident moraliser, ''Tis in ourselves that we are thus', etc. But then Shakespeare indicates his vulnerability:

If the beam of our lives had not one scale of reason to poise another of sensuality, the blood and baseness of our natures would conduct us to most prepost'rous conclusions. But we have reason to cool our raging motions, our carnal stings, our unbitted lusts.

(1.3.326–31)

Here we have self-knowledge. Here, also, we have a man who while seemingly helping and advising a friend betrays his own weaknesses.

We shall see how this pattern repeats itself so often with Roderigo. It is as though Iago *has* to get things out of his own system before coming down to offering practical advice. In this case he wants to get Roderigo to Cyprus. Why? – it is not clear. But here obviously is a young man so much in love who might be useful to Iago later on. Shakespeare does not allow a clear explanation, only 'Thus do I ever make my fool my purse.' It seems he wants Roderigo to get as much money as possible for his own means, but the rest of his first soliloquy doesn't illuminate this issue any further.

This soliloquy is easy to understand and seemingly at first glance easy to play. Here we have a laid-back villain setting out his plan of destruction – yes? – No! I noted the 'lunges' of thought and turns on a sixpence. The words 'I hate the Moor' start in the middle of a line! Not much time for a considered pause, then, after 'sport and profit'. He admits that he doesn't really know if the rumour of Emilia's affair with Othello has any truth to it. He says he will now act though as if it were true. And suddenly 'Cassio's a proper man' leaps out of his mouth. Then comes the thought of usurping Cassio's lieutenantship. But he has to ask 'How? How?' *Then*, and *only then*, comes the germination of a plan, 'to abuse Othello's ear / That he is too familiar with his wife' (lines 395–6). In describing Othello's gullibility there is a strange softness in Iago's words and I always thought that the words 'And will as tenderly be led by th' nose / As asses are' (lines 401–2) are mixed with a certain warmth as well as distaste.

But finally Iago has to admit that the plan is only 'engendered' and that 'Hell and night / Must bring this monstrous birth to the world's light' (lines 403–4). Hardly the laid-back smiling villain laying down a very sure and clear plan of action. I did note that the seed for the plan was put into Iago's head with Brabantio's parting words. Somehow his statement went into Iago's subconscious and was used. Iago's ability to take from moments or words spoken on stage and use them for his own ends recurs throughout the play.

Then comes the arrival in Cyprus, along with Emilia. Cassio, noticing Iago's reaction to his rather bold welcome to Emilia, apologises. Iago turns that immediately to a joke against his wife for the benefit of the other soldiers. Suddenly Shakespeare plunges the scene into jokes against wives and women. And it's interesting that Shakespeare allows Desdemona not only to get caught up in the game herself but to deflect the jokes aimed at Emilia on to herself. There's a wonderful piece of irony here when she admits: 'I am not merry; but I do beguile / The thing I am by seeming otherwise' (2.1.122–3). This to the greatest seemer of them all! Iago gives Desdemona a run for her money but from line 148, 'She that was ever fair' to the end of the speech, almost involuntarily he gets into lewd, dark areas of description, going even further into sexuality; he has to end with literally a (limp) impotent conclusion: 'To suckle fools and chronicle small beer.' I played that moment as if 'reason' had to be called upon here to stop him really stepping over the bounds of acceptable language to Othello's young wife. It is in this frame of mind that he notes Cassio's taking her 'by the palm' and privately (with the audience) the language does become really vulgar.

I noted also that the word 'trumpet' in 'The Moor! I know his trumpet' nearly always sounded like 'strumpet' unless I put a deliberate gap after 'his'. I pondered on Shakespeare's intentions but allowed the line its ambiguity which some audiences did pick up.

'O, you are well tuned now!' (line 199) completes Othello's half line, 'That e'er our hearts shall make' which told me that Shakespeare wanted Iago to come straight in with his line, the reason being that Iago is witnessing something beautiful, something he cannot bear to watch. This aside has always in all productions I have ever seen been played just for a laugh, but I believe that underneath the obvious surface comedy of the line lies pain and cynicism. My belief is supported by the end of Act 2, Scene 1, the second big Iago/Roderigo scene.

Instead of immediately planning the riot, Iago (pushed by Shakespeare) goes into perhaps the darkest areas of twisted, bitter, and sexual language that the play contains. I noted the following points. For Roderigo's benefit, he paints a picture of Desdemona as a lustful nyphomaniac. Don't forget that Roderigo is desperately in love with her. He dismisses Othello's power for lovemaking completely. And then comes the most surprising language about Cassio:

A knave very voluble; no further conscionable than in putting on the mere form of civil and humane seeming, for the better compassing of his salt and most hidden loose affection . . . a slipper and subtle knave; a finder-out of occasion; that has an eye can stamp and counterfeit advantages, though true advantage never present itself; a devilish knave!   (2.1.238–45)

All this about *Cassio*? I couldn't help but read the most perfect description of *himself*! And how very human that is!

Then Iago describes Cassio and Desdemona together. Here Iago goes deeper and deeper into his own sexual, almost masturbatory imagery ending up with 'th'incorporate conclusion'. Then very suddenly, as if Iago himself realises he has gone almost too far, he gets on with the plotting of the riot.

So far then, let me sum up the type of man I was beginning to see: a man who is jealous about everything – and finding particulars to justify his feelings (these particulars we know are not valid); a man whose life has changed through his general's marriage; a man who swears revenge; a soldier who makes jokes about his wife; a man who is sexually obsessed and sees life and goodness through splintered, green glasses – love is lust, courtesy is lechery, kissing hands leads not to making love but to pure fucking; a man who has caused one act of chaos (waking up of Brabantio) and is about to cause another; a man who really is confused, mixed up over one person in particular. He has openly slandered Desdemona and Cassio, but what of *Othello* – very little? *Perhaps*, and only perhaps, did it enter my mind that his jealousy could be centred around the one area he has hardly mentioned, Othello, and in particular his mind, the mind Desdemona said she fell in love with. But this is conjecture – more later. So, a pretty mixed-up, pained human being.

And now, at this point, when this very confusing picture is being drawn, Shakespeare gives Iago the most difficult and complex soliloquy that I have ever encountered. The soliloquy is full of confusion as Iago himself admits: ''Tis here; but yet confus'd' (2.1.311).

The first two lines ('That Cassio loves her, I do well believe't; / That she loves him, 'tis apt and of great credit', lines 286–7), are obviously sarcastic and cynical; the next three and a half lines present the first complexity:

> The Moor (howbeit that I endure him not)
> Is of a constant, loving, noble nature,
> And I dare think he'll prove to Desdemona
> A most dear husband.

There is no doubt (unlike the first two lines which are obviously lies) that he is uttering the truth. And I noticed how, in spite of *enduring him not*, he praises Othello's character, and hardly dares to think of the happy couple together.

Then comes the very enigmatic 'Now I do love her too.' Does he? No, of course not! Why not? Well, maybe he does? Does he? We have come full circle. But *if* he does, *this* time it is '*not* out of absolute lust'. What pain there is here if the lines are played just for their value and not for any easy cheap laugh. Once again Shakespeare lets the audience into Iago's mind, to become voyeurs to his private anguish. Next, he actually describes the pain of his jealousy (about Othello and Emilia), in pure *physical* terms:

> the thought whereof
> Doth (*like a poisonous mineral*) gnaw my inwards;
> And nothing can or shall content my soul . . .   (lines 296–8)

Hence his revenge must be satisfied in getting even, 'wife for wife', but he admits the impossibility immediately: 'Or failing so'. And then comes the big clue to the whole role:

> Or failing so, yet that I put the *Moor*
> At least into a *jealousy* so strong
> That judgment cannot cure.   (lines 300–2)

Iago then tries to plot (bring 'reason' back): 'Which thing to do', etc. Then, suddenly, a non sequitur leap of jealousy: 'For I fear Cassio with my night-cap too.' And then the extraordinary antithesis of

> Make the Moor *thank* me, *love* me, and *reward me*,
> For making him egregiously an ass,
> And practising upon *his* peace and quiet
> Even to madness. 'Tis here, but yet confus'd,
> Knavery's plain face is never seen till us'd.   (2.1.308–312)

So a most confused soliloquy – almost an admission of all the problems of love and jealousy and confusion that have driven him to a madness that won't let go. Iago has to *do* something now. The pain is too great to cope with.

At this point in the play, Shakespeare lets the audience see Iago at work – the honest Iago, the man everybody loves, the man who cannot bring the reality of private feelings into his relationships with people. Having shown what are the black depths of Iago's thought, attitude, and words, Shakespeare now paints on top the most seductive veneer of honest charm.

Note how genuine he is with Cassio (in the beginning of Act 2, Scene 3); also note how his next, short, soliloquy suddenly sounds more like direct speech to the audience, and note as well the obvious humour and warmth of 'Now, my sick fool Roderigo, / Whom love hath turn'd almost the wrong side out', etc. Now Iago is positive and suddenly everything he wants *works*. Terrific. Cassio gets drunk and in spite of Iago giving the most wonderful defence of Cassio to Othello (while at the same time obviously pointing the finger of blame right at him), Cassio has his lieutenantship taken away from him for causing a riot. Again I noticed how Iago suddenly takes the cue from what is said on stage to prompt his actions.

OTHELLO   And he that is approv'd in this offence,
          Though he had twinn'd with me, both at a birth,
          Shall *lose* me.   (2.3.211–13)

So, if Iago can subtly lay the blame on Cassio, Othello will literally 'lose' Cassio. This shows Iago's deep knowledge of Othello's character. His word is his word. How unlike Iago.

Another thing I noticed is that Iago has timed the riot at the moment when Othello and Desdemona are preparing for or in the act of lovemaking. Then Othello's offer to nurse Montano's wounds himself obviously destroys the first night together on this warm Mediterranean island. Could this have been planned? Knowing Iago's mind, anything is possible.

Iago now makes sure Cassio suspects nothing and brilliantly supports his getting his pardon by using Desdemona as the go-between. This thought could have been triggered off by Desdemona's appearance on stage, but that may be just conjecture. Cassio leaves thinking Iago is his best friend and then Shakespeare, with a stroke of genius, gives Iago a chance to play the audience as he plays with other characters. Here is a soliloquy unlike any of the others. The audience is charmed and won over by his direct address. What wonderful effrontery to be able to turn to his audience and ask 'And what's he then that says I play the villain?' The speech becomes Machiavellian towards the end, but in this soliloquy there are no doubts, no anguish. Iago is happy, almost for the first time in the play, and totally confident. He easily gets rid of Roderigo whose function dramatically, at least for now, is over. Iago has no more need of him. Who then does Iago need? He has got rid of Cassio being close to Othello and now he's going to make Othello suspect Desdemona. Is he getting rid of everyone close to Othello? A question that has to remain unanswered. It is clear, though, what he means to do:

> My wife must move for Cassio to her mistress –
> I'll set her on –
> Myself a while to draw the Moor apart,
> And bring him jump when he may Cassio find
> Soliciting his wife. (2.3.383–7)

It was at this point in our production that we took the interval.

From here on until he slips up, fate plays into Iago's hand. In the very next scene (3.1), Cassio is saying:

> I have made bold, Iago,
> To send in to your wife. My suit to her
> Is that she will to virtuous Desdemona
> Procure me some access. (3.1.33–6)

With a wry smile Iago replies 'I'll send her to you presently.' The first part of the plan is under way and some 43 lines or so later he sets the second part in motion with 'Hah? I like not that' (3.3.35). This is a very long scene with many important sections which must be discussed. The first main section runs from the beginning of the scene to line 257 and is often referred to as the first temptation scene. In a sense this is correct but slightly misleading. It is a scene which must be played dangerously, i.e. moment by moment, thought by thought, as much improvised as possible (which is how it is written). If it is played in any way calculatingly, by Iago gleefully observing Othello's grabbing the bait, it becomes comic and makes Othello look really foolish.

As in the scenes with Roderigo and Cassio, Iago must find his way into this scene with great care. He has got to be prepared to pull out of the scene if it becomes too dangerous for him to continue. Othello has to be drawn and persuaded and honestly gulled by every one of Iago's words. And every now and then Shakespeare throws us Iago's painful knowledge about himself:

> Men should be what they seem,
> Or those that be not, would they might seem none! (lines 126–7)

Although this is said for effect, the lines *cannot* be passed over, for Iago is not who he seems to be. Two lines later I played the moment (after the line, 'Why then I think Cassio's an honest man') as the final line and went to leave Othello because of this realisation of who he (Iago) is or rather who he can never be, 'true to himself'.

From here on there was a genuine resistance to Othello's pleading which I never 'arched' or made wry. And when Iago throws 'O, beware, my lord, of jealousy' at Othello and describes the pain of such a disease, who knows better than Iago these effects? So there is much more going on in this scene than pure temptation. Only when forced by Othello to 'utter [his] thoughts' and when it is relatively safe to do so, does Iago start pushing the scene into its area of cruel insinuation (from line 192); if up to this point the scene is played in a very genuine way then the rest of this section is fairly straightforward.

The next main section for Iago occurs with his wife. It is an important scene, the only one they ever have on their own and thus it must convey a full relationship, whatever that might be. Shakespeare does not make it easy, for it is not a long scene (Shylock and Jessica have a similar problem in *The Merchant of Venice*, only twenty-two lines).

Janet Dale was our Emilia and I cannot imagine a better portrayal. She played Emilia as a woman desperately needing and wanting Iago's love, and therefore one who would do anything to please him or his fantasy (sexual or otherwise); she is thus a woman who knows Iago's weaknesses and is prepared to put up with them, believing that basically he is a good man. Her confusion then when she learns about his (eventual) truly malignant doings (the constant repetition of 'My husband') is very genuine.

Janet and I played the scene together in three sections. In lines 300–4 we set up a 'used to being married' relationship. From lines 304 to 315 we played a sexual flirtation. Instead of making Iago snatch the handkerchief (which most editors like although the stage direction is not in Folio or Quarto), Emilia was almost saying 'be nice to me, kiss me, etc. and I'll give it to you'. As she brushed it past my lips I took it away from her hands by grasping it between my teeth. From lines 315 to 320, I played harsh and cruel – very cruel – and barked 'leave me' at her – leaving her to exit bewildered and sad.

I then faced another soliloquy which once more opened up Iago's sexual torment. *Why*, I kept wondering, doesn't Shakespeare end the speech after Iago announces his intention, 'I will in Cassio's lodging lose this napkin, /

And let him find it' (lines 321–2)? The rest of the soliloquy doesn't tell us any more about what will happen next – only 'This may do something'.

I realised that something was happening to Iago now that he has this handkerchief. He once more describes the physical pain of jealousy:

> Dangerous conceits are in their natures poisons,
> Which at the first are scarce found to distaste,
> But with a little act upon the blood
> Burn like the mines of sulphur. (lines 326–9)

This reminded me of the sixteenth-century description: 'The envious body is constrained to bite on his bridle, to chew and devour his envy within himself and to lock up his own misery in his heart; this causeth great stomach pain.' (I found this quotation in *The Masks of Othello* by Marvin Rosenberg – a book which helped me a great deal.) Just before 'trifles light as air' I laid the handkerchief gently over my face and then blew it up into the air. Gradually this 'trifle' turned into the 'dangerous conceit' and ended up screwed tight in my hand – no longer a trifle but the cause of great pain. 'I did say so' was therefore said as an acknowledgement of this fact.

The final section in this 'marathon' scene, from lines 330 to 480, is the most dangerous scene for Iago and I noticed that he only has six lines, compared to forty for Othello. Ben grabbed my throat on 'Villain, be sure thou prove my love a whore' (line 359) and only let go after 'For nothing canst thou to damnation add / Greater than that' (lines 372–3).

Grabbing this opportunity, I played the next section very aggressively and very hurt. How could he, Othello, even think of treating me like that! From then on I played Iago on the attack right up until line 431. Nestled snugly among those lines is the 'I lay with Cassio lately' speech. Did he? Didn't he? More questions and more ambiguities. First, if he didn't, why bring it up? There was no reason to lie with Cassio as he has lodgings with Emilia and in any case there was no time for him to do so – we know he hasn't slept since arriving in Cyprus. In fact there is no evidence that Iago is telling the truth.

But whether Iago did or didn't (and I don't believe he did), Othello never questions the possibility. One can argue that he's incensed with jealous thoughts by now but I believe there's more to it than that. I noticed that before launching into the story, Iago says 'Prick'd to't by foolish honesty and *love*, / I will go on' (lines 412–13). Here questions about Iago's sexuality arise. He is about to embark on a homosexual image about himself and Cassio, at the same time making Othello more jealous about

33   Iago and Othello (Ben Kingsley) in Act 4, Scene 1

Cassio and Desdemona, and prefacing the whole thing with 'I am only going to do this because I love you.'

After this speech, Shakespeare brings Othello and Iago together in a symbolic 'marriage', with both men calling upon supernatural powers to help 'their' revenge. Othello completely dismisses his love for Desdemona: 'All my fond love thus do I blow to heaven. / 'Tis gone' (lines 445–6). Iago swears to help Othello in 'What bloody work so ever' (Quarto reading). Othello replies with 'I greet thy *love*' and then suggests putting Cassio to death. Fairly straightforward, I thought, until Iago's reply caught me unawares by its homosexual suggestion, 'My *friend* is dead' – homosexual in the context of 'I lay with Cassio lately.' I also find it interesting that to put *Cassio* to death is Othello's first job for Iago. Yes, obviously, because of jealousy – but could it be *double* jealousy – the fact that Cassio went to bed with Iago as well as what he said to Desdemona/Iago? Certainly, as I previously mentioned, Othello never questions the possibility of an Iago/ Cassio liaison. How much then does Othello know of Iago's bisexuality or homosexuality? What is their past? These are bombshell questions, never directly answered, open to suppositions. It's interesting though that after Othello suggests killing Desdemona also, he comes out with 'Now art thou my lieutenant' (line 479). How long has Othello been aware of Iago's pain at not being lieutenant in the first place? It suddenly throws light on the truth of the opening scene of the play. Obviously with Desdemona as a new bride Iago was just not classy enough, but now that she is as good as dead, Iago is promoted.

I also noted the ambiguity of the response, 'I am your own for ever.' On a simplistic level it means what is most obvious – I will be your lieutenant for ever, but in light of the already discussed complexities, it also takes on the sense of a far deeper bonding of two men for life. Is Iago then a homosexual, bisexual, or what? Shakespeare never tells us but only suggests. I did feel though that to play the *ambiguity* was true to the scene.

When we see Iago again (in Act 3, Scene 4, after a five minute 'rest') he is truly evil and hateful: no subtlety in this scene, just plain double-dealing. What gall! I thought that this scene has to alienate the audience as it is so blatant. We may not see the subtle Iago, but there is one lovely dig at Cassio when he mentions how well he knows Othello as a soldier (fighting man) – of course it reminds us of 'Preferment goes by letter and affection / And not by old gradation.' The scene is basically one of Iago pretending that he is surprised that Othello is angry. But on another, deeper, level, it gives Iago the information that Othello is showing his anger *publicly*, i.e. he's taken the bait.

And the next time we see Iago at work (Act 4, Scene 1) we realise the bait has been swallowed whole. Iago is fanning the fire of jealousy now burning in Othello's body and mind. Othello seemingly now *wants* to be told the worst and never even questions the 'facts' given by Iago. Once he's heard Iago assert that Cassio did 'lie – with her. On her; what you will' Othello has his 'fit'. Epileptic? I don't think so. I think it's another one of Iago's great 'cover-ups'. The true clinical symptoms of epilepsy are clearly *not* being shown by Othello because Iago tells Cassio that if he (Cassio) touches Othello they *will* start. Also we have seen no indication of his fit 'yesterday'. No, for whatever reason Othello has fainted (hyperventilation caused by extreme jealousy?); it is *not* something that is a common occurrence.

The time on stage between the beginning of Othello's unconscious state and Cassio's entrance, lines 44–8, is, for me, perhaps one of the most important moments of the whole play, because it is the *only* time Iago is on stage with Othello when the latter is unable to react. Hence it is a private moment for Iago in the *presence* of Othello:

> Work on,
> My medicine, work! Thus credulous fools are caught,
> And many worthy and chaste dames even thus
> (All guiltless) meet reproach. – What ho! my lord!
> My lord, I say! Othello!   (4.1.44–8)

I was obviously aware of the gloating over his own achievement, but I noticed also that he uses a *female* image. Then there are the three addresses to Othello. Why bother to separate these phrases? Because of all the complexities of their relationship that I had discovered previous to this moment, it was impossible to ignore the movement from gloating over a supine defenceless body to the use of the name 'Othello'. It suggested love and hate very close together. 'What ho! my lord!' was to bring him round, 'My lord, I say!' was showing concern about his physical state, and 'Othello!' was said cradling him in my arms, feeling sorry for the man I was destroying. This led very comfortably into 'No, forbear' to Cassio, in other words, 'don't you dare touch him!' And that led into a show of relief with 'Look, he stirs.' Having got Cassio to leave the stage, Iago then endeavours to get Othello to rally round by, once again, Shakespeare's use of aided soliloquy (Othello has seven lines to Iago's thirty-two). Iago gives his bitterly sexual and misogynistic view of relationships. I stressed the bitter irony of 'And knowing what I am, I know what she [Quarto] shall be' (line 73). Another thing I noticed was the repetition of 'man':

Would you would bear your fortune like a man!	(line 61)
Good sir, be a man.	(line 65)
A passion most unsuiting such a man.	(line 77)
And nothing of a man.	(line 89)

Iago cannot bear 'weak' men, obviously!

I noted also the sarcasm in 'I shifted him [Cassio] away / And laid good 'scuse upon your *ecstasy*' (lines 78–9). Here also is a hint that Othello's fit was not epileptic – if it *was* then why not tell Othello what he told to Cassio?

The next section, where Othello overhears what Iago and Cassio are saying, relies upon the audience's willingness to believe the situation more than anything else. True theatre licence! What is worth noting in Cassio's character, however, is the fact that he never even asks Iago how Othello is – extraordinarily selfish, I thought! This scene ultimately convinces Othello, and Shakespeare tops it all by having Bianca come on and produce *the handkerchief*. In a sense, Iago needn't do anything else to persuade Othello. It has been done for him.

Apart from the oscillations of Othello's love and hate and a few more nudges from Iago such as 'If you are so fond over her iniquity, give her patent to offend, for if it touch not you, it comes near nobody' (lines 197–9), the next part of the plot is hatched. It is Othello who now suggests, 'Get me some poison, Iago, this night' (line 204). Iago, though, is quick to react (cautious that poison in itself may fail) and suggests 'Do it not with poison; strangle her in her bed, even the bed she has contaminated.' Then Iago even gets permission to kill Cassio, 'And for Cassio, let me be his undertaker.' It's vital to Iago that Cassio dies. It is vital that Desdemona dies also – *both* dead.

Fate plays into Iago's hand again. Lodovico comes from Venice and allows Iago to say ''Tis Lodovico – This comes from the Duke. See, your wife's with *him*!' (lines 214–15). Lodovico tells that Othello has been called back to Venice and Cassio is 'to take his place' (Iago uses this information with Roderigo later). And witness the crazed behaviour of Othello with Desdemona. Othello strikes her, rants and raves, etc., causing Lodovico to exclaim (after Othello and Desdemona have left): 'Is this the noble Moor whom our full Senate / Call all in all sufficient?' (lines 264–5). Again, this section from here to the end of the scene could easily be played for laughs but that would make nonsense of Lodovico and the seriousness of the action. I played it absolutely straight, showing that I was as distressed as Lodovico was. Lodovico and Iago exit, and Iago has another earned *rest*! This long scene, though, presented many challenges to me. It required very quick thinking on my feet – the complexity of my private moment with Othello (unconscious), the plot setting with Cassio, the sealing of the proof for Othello, and finally, the setting up of two deaths (Cassio's and Desdemona's) and getting Lodovico to see Othello in a very different light.

Iago returns in Act 4, Scene 2, this time at Desdemona's bidding. She wants to know 'What shall I do to win my lord again?' (line 149). This scene could also be played for cheap laughs but that would make a mockery of Desdemona's character. I played genuine concern all the way through the scene. There is, however, ironic humour in lines like 'Fie, there is no such man; it is impossible' coming straight after Emilia's 'I will be hang'd if . . . / Some cogging, cozening slave, to get some office, / Have not devis'd this slander. I will be hang'd else' (lines 130–3). But within this short scene Shakespeare gets rid of all doubt as to whether there is any truth in the rumour that she had had an affair with Othello. No woman would ever say, in the presence of the Moor's *wife*:

> Some such squire he was
> That turn'd your wit the seamy side without,
> And made you to suspect me with the Moor.   (lines 145–7)

Iago quite rightly replies, 'You are a fool, go to'. In other words, 'How can you bring that subject up at a time like this?'

He tells Desdemona not to worry at all – ''tis but his humour. / The business of the state does him offence, / And he does chide with you' (lines 165–7) – and ushers her and Emilia off the stage – on to which walks someone we have not seen for ages, and I put that same feeling into 'How now, *Roderigo*' (line 172). But now the first real threat to Iago occurs. Roderigo has changed from a romantic lover into a disillusioned man, very angry at and suspicious about Iago, a man who challenges him: 'I will seek satisfaction of you' (line 199). I played genuine surprise and fear at Roderigo's behaviour, but realised there was a way I could use him. My Roderigo, Gerard Logan, showed that in spite of all, he still loved Desdemona and allowed himself to be convinced that he should kill Cassio. Roderigo has mostly been played as just an upper-class fool, but Gerard's interpretation of the true 'romantic lover' opened up many new areas of the part.

Another rest for Iago before returning in Act 5, Scene 1, when things start to go wrong for him. The plot to kill Cassio fails – Roderigo misses! Iago wounds Cassio and comes back to finish the deed only to find Lodovico and Gratiano there. Cassio should and must die but Iago can't, because of the situation, do this. In order to save his own skin he kills Roderigo and uses the arrival of Bianca to get out of a very nasty situation indeed. I played off Bianca in a very cruel fashion and by doing so convinced Lodovico she was guilty of starting the fray.

Almost immediately Iago makes a major mistake. Without thinking, he says to Emilia: 'Run you to the citadel / And tell my lord and lady what hath happ'd' (lines 126–7). He completely forgets that Othello should be killing or have killed Desdemona. I played the realisation of what I had done immediately which led into the aside, 'This is the night / That either makes me or fordoes me quite.' It could be argued that Iago deliberately sends Emilia to Othello in order to stop the murder. But Iago wouldn't gain anything by that. He would have to start all over again and if that was the case, why didn't he go himself? Once again Iago's complexities emerge. It could even be argued that there's a self-destruct button that Iago plays with all the time and gets excited at the prospect of pressing it – both excited and afraid.

The audience sees Othello then kill Desdemona, witnesses Emilia's realisation that Othello has murdered Desdemona and that her husband was involved in the rumour of Desdemona's adultery with Cassio, and then sees Iago himself come on to the stage to be challenged by his wife to 'Disprove this villain, if thou be'st a man' (5.2.172). Iago, amazingly, says what he has done, dismisses his wife's ravings as mad, and tries to get her to go home. But when Emilia admits to stealing the handkerchief Iago knows that his game is up. From being the most voluble person in the play he goes to weak expletives, 'Villainous whore', 'Filth, thou liest.' The time for talk is over; in the last scene of the play Iago has only two and half lines. He kills his wife and runs out. This action seals his guilt and fate. The self-destruct button is now pushed fully home.

When Iago is brought back in, Othello tries to kill him but fails – why? It is a most important point. Physically Othello could kill him easily but somehow he can't do it. I believe that Othello literally *can't* kill the man who loves him and this is how Ben Kingsley and I played the moment. This allowed me to utter my last lines quite differently from the conventional defiant shout. I implied that he mustn't ask why I did what I did – because in truth he really *knows* and that I will not tell anyone the truth, not even under all the tortures in the world. Ben Kingsley then directed 'Well, thou dost best' (line 306) at me, so that we both understood.

Othello's only exit now is suicide but it's the one Iago least suspects will happen. And when it did, I threw myself on his dying body only to be pulled off by guards. I did this for two reasons: first, shock and surprise at Othello's suicide and second, to follow the hate/love theme right through to the end.

What did Iago achieve by these killings? Before Othello's suicide the answer would have been *Othello himself*, freed from marriage – as he was before the play started. I realised that Iago has got rid of everyone close to him and Othello – Emilia, Roderigo, Desdemona and an attempted murder of Cassio. Iago's failure to kill Cassio undid him. Othello killing himself destroys him. There's nothing left.

The most deadly, confused, jealous psychopath leaves to be tortured. Will he speak up? I don't think so. He will stay true to the man he hated and loved at one and the same time.

So, who is Iago, what is he? Is he a simple 'label'? In this 'supermarket' world of ours it's hardly surprising that he has been labelled. But I chose not to label. My 'jar' is just called Iago with one main ingredient – Jealousy. He is illogical (true to human nature) and dangerous. As we despise Iago, we like him; as we think we know him, somehow we feel sorry for this murderer. Why? Because Iago – Jack, *plain* Jack – is in all of us, could be any one of us, could even be you.

Production credits

Productions have been listed in the order of this book's chapters. With the exception of the 1984 *Romeo and Juliet*, which closed at Stratford after a national tour, all were first presented at the Royal Shakespeare Theatre (RST) at Stratford, and (except for *The Merchant of Venice*) they were subsequently seen at the Barbican Theatre in London. All productions, with the exception of those staged at Stratford in 1985, were also performed in Newcastle upon Tyne after the end of their respective Stratford seasons. The date given is that of their first public performance at Stratford. Further details can conveniently be found in the RSC's *Yearbooks*.

MEASURE FOR MEASURE
RST, 29 September 1983
Director – Adrian Noble
Design and costumes – Bob Crowley
Music – Ilona Sekacz
Lighting – Robert Bryan

LOVE'S LABOUR'S LOST
RST, 4 October 1984
Director – Barry Kyle
Design and costumes – Bob Crowley
Music – Guy Woolfenden
Lighting – Chris Ellis

THE MERCHANT OF VENICE
RST, 5 April 1984
Director – John Caird
Design and costumes – Ultz
Music – Ilona Sekacz
Lighting – Robert Bryan

AS YOU LIKE IT
RST, 11 April 1985
Director – Adrian Noble
Design and costumes – Bob Crowley
Music – Howard Blake
Lighting – David Hersey

TWELFTH NIGHT
RST, 14 April 1983
Director – John Caird
Designer – Robin Don
Costumes – Alix Stone
Music – Ilona Sekacz
Lighting – David Hersey

HENRY V
RST, 22 March 1984
Director – Adrian Noble
Design and costumes – Bob Crowley
Music – Howard Blake
Lighting – Robert Bryan

ROMEO AND JULIET
The Other Place, 25 April 1984
(after a tour beginning in Lincoln, 10 October 1983)
Director – John Caird
Designer – Bob Crowley
Costumes – Priscilla Truett
Music – Ilona Sekacz
Lighting – Brian Harris

ROMEO AND JULIET
RST, 31 March 1986
Director – Michael Bogdanov
Designer – Chris Dyer
Costumes – Chris Dyer and Ginny Humphreys
Music – Sato Hiroshi
Lighting – Chris Ellis

HAMLET
RST, 9 August 1984
Director – Ron Daniels
Design and costumes – Maria Bjornson
Music – Nigel Hess
Lighting – Chris Ellis

KING LEAR
RST, 10 June 1982
Director – Adrian Noble
Design and costumes – Bob Crowley
Music – Ilona Sekacz
Lighting – Robert Bryan

OTHELLO
RST, 19 September 1985
Director – Terry Hands
Designer – Ralph Koltai
Costumes – Alexander Reid
Music – Nigel Hess
Lighting – Terry Hands and Clive Morris

Further reading

Sally Beauman's *The Royal Shakespeare Company. A History of Ten Decades* (Oxford, 1980) supersedes earlier accounts of its subject. Description and commentary on major productions by the Company will be found in Stanley Wells's *Royal Shakespeare* (Manchester, 1977) and Richard David's *Shakespeare in the Theatre* (Cambridge, 1978); see also Ralph Berry, *Changing Styles in Shakespeare* (1981). Clive Priestley's *Financial Scrutiny of the Royal Shakespeare Company*, published by Her Majesty's Stationery Office (two volumes in one, 1984), contains invaluable background material on the Company's operating practices and budgeting. Work at The Pit and The Other Place is discussed in Colin Chambers's *Other Spaces* (1980).

Antony Sher, in *The Year of the King: An Actor's Diary and Sketchbook* (1985), gives a vivid description of preparations for a Stratford production (*Richard III* in 1984) from the leading actor's point of view. As well as conveying his own attitudes to rehearsal and performance, John Barton's *Playing Shakespeare* (1985) includes comments on their methods and on past performances by a number of RSC actors, including David Suchet and Ben Kingsley.

The RSC's *Yearbooks* (published retrospectively, season-by-season, since 1978) bring together photographs, essays, statistics, and – especially useful – resumés of press reactions to productions. The RSC's position as a national cultural institution is questioned by Alan Sinfield in an essay included in *Political Shakespeare* (edited by Jonathan Dollimore and Alan Sinfield, Manchester, 1985). A trenchant article by Andrew Rissik on RSC verse-speaking and voice production will be found in *New Theatre Quarterly*, 1, 3 (1985). The head of the RSC's Voice Department, Cicely Berry, frequently referred to in the preceding essays, published her *The Actor and his Text* in 1987. Among academic journals offering detailed critical accounts of each season's productions are *Shakespeare Survey* (Cambridge, annually), *Shakespeare Quarterly* (Washington), and *Cahiers Elisabéthains* (Montpellier).